Popular Culture as Art and Knowledge

Popular Culture as Art and Knowledge

A Critique of Authoritarian Neoliberalism and the Crisis of Democracy

George A. Gonzalez

LEXINGTON BOOKS
Lanham • Boulder • New York • London

Published by Lexington Books
An imprint of The Rowman & Littlefield Publishing Group, Inc.
4501 Forbes Boulevard, Suite 200, Lanham, Maryland 20706
www.rowman.com

6 Tinworth Street, London SE11 5AL, United Kingdom

British Library Cataloguing in Publication Information Available

Library of Congress Cataloging-in-Publication Data Available

ISBN 978-1-4985-8977-2 (cloth)
ISBN 978-1-4985-8979-6 (pbk)
ISBN 978-1-4985-8978-9 (electronic)

For Ileana and Alana

Contents

Introduction

This volume takes up the debate between analytic and continental philosophy. I turn to art, more specifically popular culture, to demonstrate the validity of continental philosophy. This is my third book drawing on popular culture to make an argument for continental philosophy. The first two books are titled *The Absolute and Star Trek* and *Star Trek and the Politics of Globalism*,[1] and as the titles suggest I rely entirely on the Star Trek franchise in these books. In the current volume I continue to utilize the Star Trek text, but I also use a number of other episodic broadcast series, including *Game of Thrones*, *Veep*, *House of Cards*, and *Making a Murderer* (among others).

Drawing on the philosophy of Georg Hegel (perhaps the most important of continental philosophers), James Kreines holds that *reason in the world* metaphysically exists.[2] *Reasons of the world* are reasons of the Hegelian Absolute. Thus, similar to the fact that gravity is curves in the space-time continuum along which matter moves[3]—reasons are the grooves in the Absolute along which human decision-making occurs. Art allows us to conceptualize, understand, speculate about the grooves (reasons) of the Absolute.

Two key points can be drawn from Kreines's position: first, normative values are embedded in reality. Thus, in complete contradistinction to analytic philosophy, there is no bifurcation between the empirical and the normative—to exist is to have normative value. Secondly, the role of social science is to cogitate, explore, identify the reasons of the world that shape social, political norms. Such an approach would decisively move the social sciences away from an emphasis on statistically significant patterns of human behavior (e.g., voting studies) and toward an approach that seeks to analyze the reasons of the world that motivate/shape social and political decisions. Art (particularly popular culture) becomes an important source in identifying the way that people reason about the world and how they perceive political elites reasoning in the world.

To adjudicate between continental and analytic philosophy I on rely on the broadcast iterations of Star Trek, as well as Nazi cinema. With regard to contemporary American politics, in addition to Star Trek, I draw on the television series *Game of Thrones*, *Veep*, *House of Cards*, and *The Man in the High Castle*. Popular culture is germane to philosophy and contemporary politics because television/movie creators frequently try to attract viewers by conveying *authentic* philosophical and political motifs. Conversely, viewers seek out *authentic* movies and television shows. This is in contrast to opinion surveys (for instance), as the formation of the data begins with the surveyor seeking to directly solicit an opinion—however impromptu or shallow.

OVERVIEW OF BOOK

Deconstruction is arguably the opposite tack to a Hegalian approach to literary criticism. The former ostensibly dismantles, obfuscates reason(s) in art—whereas the latter seeks to identify it. This effort to dismantle reason(s) in art renders deconstruction (as literary theory) similar to analytic philosophy (chapter 1). As for the hidden, sinister agendas hidden in art (as purported by deconstructionists), art reflects the biases only of the Absolute. This is evident in Nazi cinema—where the Nazis could not artistically convey their vile agenda (despite their strong desire to do so) (chapter 2). Chapters 3, 4, 5, and 6 take up philosophical issues. Relying on the Star Trek franchise, we gain answers to key questions that point to the validity of continental philosophy and most specifically Hegel's philosophy regarding the Absolute. Thus Star Trek provides prime insights into matters of the human mind, ageing (death), justice, love, instrumental reason, and the ontology of things. In chapter six, utilizing the *Dirty Harry* franchise and the Netflix series *Making a Murderer*, I describe (criminal) justice as dialectical process—where the forces of vengeance and deterrence must be countervailed by forces seeking to protect the rights of criminal defendants. In chapters 7 and 8, I change gears and focus on contemporary American politics. Television series like *House of Cards* and *The Man in the High Castle* point to an increasingly authoritarian and dangerous American politics—with war, torture, and assassination (as state policy) becoming the norm. *Veep*, *Game of Thrones*, and *House of Cards* all indicate that American democracy is in profound crisis.

NOTES

1. George A. Gonzalez, *The Absolute and Star Trek* (New York: Palgrave Macmillan, 2017), and *Star Trek and the Politics of Globalism* (New York: Palgrave Macmillan, 2018).

2. James Kreines, *Reason in the World: Hegel's Metaphysics and Its Philosophical Appeal* (New York: Oxford University Press, 2015).

3. A. Zee, *Einstein Gravity in a Nutshell* (Princeton: Princeton University Press, 2013).

Chapter One

Deconstruction versus Reason in the World

The Hegelian understanding of art creates an approach to art/literary criticism distinct from and in opposition to that of deconstruction. The ostensive purpose of deconstruction is to dismantle our understanding of reason as manifest through art—in all its forms.[1] Marc Redfield, sympathetic chronicler of the deconstruction movement during its high point at Yale University, puts it directly when he notes (in part quoting the American dean of deconstructionism Paul de Man) that deconstruction "deconstructs aesthetics as 'a phenomenalism of a process of meaning and understanding.'"[2] Thus, the purpose of deconstruction is to challenge, disrupt our understanding of art as a conveyor and depiction of reasons of the world—that is, as "a process of meaning and understanding." Simon Critchley holds that there is something of an ethical imperative to deconstructing texts as the cultural biases inherent in texts (including art) preclude real understanding across cultures.[3] Again drawing on Redfield (in part quoting de Man), deconstructionism "exposes the fallacies of an educational program in which scripted contact with literary texts is taken to promote 'the integrity of a social and historical self.'"[4]

Therefore, there is seemingly within deconstruction the assumption that in art and conventional understandings of art there are some set of unseen (often nefarious) biases that must be neutralized, or at a minimum exposed. This attitude opens deconstructionism to the charge that its adherents are excessively (hyper-) captious and ultimately nihilists—as everything is ostensibly corrupt and nothing yields coherent (unbiased, undamaged) meaning.

Two noteworthy and instructive instances of the deconstruction of aesthetics are Timothy Luke's treatment of paintings of the Old American West and Daniel Bernardi's approach to the Star Trek franchise. In both instances, readers of these cases of deconstruction are given negativity (even stigma) and obstacles to a constructive understanding of art.

1

ART AND THE AMERICAN WEST IN THE 19TH CENTURY

Luke takes issue with paintings that celebrate the integration of the American West into the broader economy during the mid to late 19th century.[5] These paintings emphasize (romanticize) economic activity (e.g., labor) in the bucolic, mountainous, forested settings of the Old West. Luke also laments the fact that Native Americans are depicted victimizing settlers—seemingly stoking hostility and hate. Luke complains that these paintings collectively ignore the realities of the Old West—the environmental exploitation, the class conflict, the mistreatment and abuse of Native Americans, and how the West was linked to finance capital in the East.[6] Luke indicates that these paintings amount to little more than propaganda, and they were used that way in the 1980s as part of the ideological resurgence of the conservative right under the auspices of President Ronald Reagan.

Significantly, Luke suggests that his analysis of these paintings lauding the colonization of the U.S. West is inspired by Karl Marx, and other related thinkers.[7] Marx, at best, is a dubious figure to invoke in a critique of what can be described as the modernization of the Old West. Marx was certainly in favor of modernization—and the triumph of modernism over premodernism (like that of Native Americans).[8] Viewing the paintings that Luke critiques through the prism of modernism (and Marx), these works are celebrating the extension of the Enlightenment to farther reaches of the planet, with the progressive implications of such an expansion.[9]

No doubt the incorporation of the American West into the national and international economy should have been done with much more care (humaneness) for the environment, workers, and, perhaps especially, for Native Americans. Certainly, any collection/exhibit of Old West art that ignores these issues is clearly deficient. Nevertheless, Luke takes his argument too far when he *deconstructs* the paintings of his study and indicates they're stealth pro-capitalist, pro-European messages. Such a conclusion places these works outside of art and into the realm of propaganda.

Looking at the politics of Luke's painting, they are presumably more progressive (pro-Enlightenment) than the traditional fare of European paintings—religious scenes (the Annunciation; the Adoration of the Magi; the Crucifixion, the Lamentation, etc.) and Greek/Roman mythology. The paintings Luke critiques have the virtue of being about human affairs and through them people can think further about these affairs. Thus, these painting may very well prompt/inspire others to inquire about the "realities" of the Old West. They may lead other painters to explore/depict the "dark" underside of the incorporation of the West into the national/international economy.

Obviously, as already alluded to, Luke is correct that the colonization of the West had an ugly side, but (as also alluded to) it also had its progressive elements. Luke appears to argue that the positive elements should be ignored. In this way he takes a similar tack to those he criticizes—only focusing on that aspect of the Old West that comports to one's biases. Worst yet, Luke's deconstruction of these paintings would have his readers believe that only brutality, venality, and environmental destruction were the values that underlaid the colonization of the American West. Again, these values were certainly present and in more than a few instances were pronounced and glaring. Nevertheless, such a vilification of the entire project of incorporating the West into the modern economy is a gross distortion. Moreover, it is demoralizing. Thus, deconstruction, far from enhancing knowledge, disseminates a distorted and corrosive view of reality.

What about the paintings depicting Native Americans assailing European settlers? Are these paintings propaganda? I would argue no. This is for two reasons. First, viewers of these paintings most likely understand the motivation of Native American violence toward settlers. Native American lands were appropriated and atrocities were committed against them. Second, while certainly some viewers of these paintings will rely on such images to argue the necessity of meting out more violence against Native Americans, other (seemingly more objective) observers can reasonably conclude that as long as Native Americans were being treated unfairly such retaliatory violence is the logical outcome.

Luke is rather misguided (or goes overboard) in deconstructing paintings (works of art) of the Old West. Nevertheless, he is engaging a political project sponsored by the conservative right that was ostensibly deliberately attempting to offer a skewed portrayal of the Old West. In the case of Daniel Bernardi he deconstructs arguably the most progressive text of the modern era—the broadcast iterations of Star Trek.

BERNARDI'S DECONSTRUCTION OF STAR TREK

One critique of deconstruction as literary criticism is that does not offer a coherent, consistent methodology. Thus, writers deconstructing a work can go about doing so as they please.[10] Daniel Bernardi invokes images and text that sustain his biases but arbitrarily ignores text and imagery in the Star Trek franchise that seemingly challenge those biases. Bernardi's book on the franchise is titled *Star Trek and History: Race-ing Toward a White Future*.[11] He claims the franchise is racist as well as sexist.

A good example of Bernardi's selective, arbitrary (self-serving) approach to the Star Trek text is his treatment of the *Next Generation* (1987–1994) character Worf (played by an African American actor). Worf, who is head of security on the star ship Enterprise, is described by Bernardi as a guard dog. In misplaced (racist[?]) language, Bernardi makes the following distastefully worded observation: Worf "is trained and domesticated, becoming . . . a trusted officer who faithfully protects the Enterprise and its white captain."[12] Why focus on Worf and not the chief engineer, who is also played by an African American actor? Bernardi does not explain. Also, why does Bernardi entirely ignore the commander of the Deep Space Nine space station in his treatment of race in the Star Trek franchise?—played by an African American actor. *Deep Space Nine* (1993–1999) began airing years before Bernardi's book was released (in 1998).

In another instance Bernardi points to the positions that the lead female characters on *Next Generation* held (Deanna Troi is the ship's counselor and Beverly Crusher is the ship's doctor): "Women in *The Next Generation* are consistently positioned as either helpers or fetishized objects. This is the case with both Dr. Crusher and Counselor Troi—their Federation jobs are supportive of their role as nurturers. The doctor and the counselor rarely give orders and almost always serve men."[13] It is noteworthy that *Next Generation* throughout numerous episodes had female actors play admirals, political leaders, and researchers. Nevertheless, it is important to note that Crusher and Troi were both senior officers—Crusher the chief medical officer and Troi the ship's psychologist as well as a lead advisor to Captain Picard. It is not entirely clear why Bernardi would choose to label them "nurturers"—as if they held the position of nannies (a position of great dignity and importance, I'll add). Additionally, I will note that all the *Next Generation* characters sustained and nurtured one another. This was part of the allure of the show.

Moreover, the Star Trek series *Voyager* (1995–2001) had a female captain. In *Deep Space Nine* the first officer and science officer were both played by women. Nevertheless, for unexplained reasons Bernardi makes his case of sexism against the franchise by relying almost entirely on the Troi and Crusher characters.

He also invokes the character of Lt. Uhura from the original series to support his claim of sexism. Bernardi makes much of the fact that Uhura's character was reduced to a bit character, given almost exclusively throwaway lines. Nevertheless, Bernardi ignores the imagery of having a bridge officer on the Enterprise during the original series (1966–1969) who is both an African American and a woman.

Bernardi is also completely arbitrary in deciding to rely on imagery or text in his indictment of Star Trek. He makes a mountain out of a molehill by pointing out that a being that is conveyed as an evolutionary advancement is glowing white ("Transfigurations" 1990), while the beings from which all humanoids evolved have a tone that is tinged brown ("The Chase" 1993): "What is striking about 'Lucy' [the representation of the original humanoid species] is that the common ancestor to the bipeds of the universe is brown. Though dark or even colored is not where we're going . . . it is apparently where we come from."[14] Bernardi goes on: "the course of evolution, of advancement and sophistication, is literally and metaphorically, physically and socially, white . . . that's . . . *The Next Generation's* version of the promised land."[15]

While Bernardi homes in on the imagery in "Transfigurations" and "The Chase", he ignores the text of these episodes, and specifically the universality communicated in them. In "Transfigurations," for instance, the alien that is going through a metamorphosis to a higher state of existence comments positively on the heterogenous composition of the Enterprise crew: "They're all so different from one another yet they work together freely. . . . Truly remarkable." The original humanoid species (in "The Chase") was very highly advanced (even with their tanned skin tone): "Life evolved on my planet before all others in this part of the galaxy. We left our world, explored the stars." Lucy preaches solidarity and unity—emphasizing that all humanoids share a common genetic basis:

> Our scientists seeded the primordial oceans of many worlds, where life was in its infancy. The seed codes directed your evolution toward a physical form resembling ours. This body you see before you, which is, of course, shaped as yours is shaped, for you are the end result. . . . It was our hope that you would have to come together in fellowship and companionship to hear this message [sent from the past in the form of Lucy]. And if you can see and hear me, our hope has been fulfilled. You are a monument, not to our greatness, but to our existence. That was our wish, that you too would know life, and would keep alive our memory. There is something of us in each of you, and so, something of you in each other. Remember us.

Lucy's message had a positive effect on a Romulan officer present during her speech. After everyone returns to their ship, he contacts Captain Picard: "It would seem that we are not completely dissimilar after all, in our hopes, or in our fears"—in spite of the current Romulan/Federation geopolitical competition. Picard: "Yes." Romulan: "Well, then. Perhaps, one day"—we can unify. Picard: "One day." Bernardi is seemingly too caught up in a game of *gotcha* to meaningfully engage the Star Trek text and its political/social implications.

While he ignores the text of certain episodes, Bernardi invokes the Star Trek text in other instances. Thus, he points to the following line in the *Next Generation* 1989 episode "The Icarus Factor": "there is, of course, a genetic predisposition toward hostility among all Klingons." Again, why invoke this bit of text but yet overlook Lucy's speech or John Doe's observation of the well-integrated Enterprise crew? Bernardi uses this line about the Klingons to smear the Star Trek franchise as racist: "Such a notion has informed real-world studies from social Darwinism and eugenics to today's neoconservative books as *The Bell Curve*."[16]

In *The Politics of Star Trek*, I hold, relying on a broad reading of the franchise text, that this line about the Klingons (who have dark skin and dark wavy hair) is in actuality about American perceptions of Arab politics:

> Reading the Klingons as Arabs could allow the viewer to have a positive take on the claim that the former have "a genetic predisposition toward hostility." In a literary/artistic sense, for Arabs this statement could be viewed as a *badge of honor*. This is because Arabs, for centuries, have been a conquered people (the Ottoman Empire and the European mandates after World War One); dominated by corrupt/repressive regimes; and suffered a diaspora with the creation of Israel and the humiliation of occupation (i.e., the West Bank Territories and the Gaza Strip). In the American Mind Arabs have been inherently (i.e., genetically[?]) unwilling to suffer these conditions passively, and responded with violent resistance (including suicide bombings). (In "Reunion" [*Next Generation*—1990] a Klingon carries out a suicide attack—with a bomb implanted inside his arm.) Perhaps all of us would like to believe that our identity group has "a genetic predisposition toward hostility" against regimes of perpetual repression/injustice/occupation.[17]

Without suggesting that my interpretation is justified or not, it does have the virtue of trying to make sense of the line concerning the genetic predisposition of Klingons within the context of the franchise and the many statements it makes about ethnicity. Bernardi, in contrast, seeks to deconstruct Star Trek—which literally means destroying/stigmatizing it.

I also hold that the line about Klingons having "a genetic predisposition toward hostility" can be read as a commentary about how the nationalism embedded in nation-states predisposes societies throughout the world to hostilities toward other nation-states. I make the point that "In a literal sense, with a nation-state system governing the world, humans do have *a genetic propensity toward hostility* [other nations (nationalism)]—as information about national identity (e.g.,'Hispanic') is regularly compiled/collected along with actual genetically driven characteristics (e.g., gender)."[18] Taking the Star Trek text as a whole, this interpretation is seemingly fairer than Bernardi's—who, again, is ostensibly more interested in playing a game of *gotcha* than analyzing the franchise in a full-faith manner.

I would submit that my treatment of Star Trek is attractive precisely because I try to find meaning in the franchise—as opposed to seeking to dismantle (deconstruct) it, as Bernardi does. By trying to find meaning (below) in the Star Trek text (its broadcast iterations) I find Hegel and Marx. A profound problem with deconstructionism is that its adherents don't seek out meaning in texts but instead try to dismantle any meaning in said texts, or argue that the meaning/biases in texts are somehow nefarious.

Analytic philosophy takes a similar tack, insofar that its proponents hold that a value-free reality exists but people cannot overcome their biases to see it. I challenge this metaphysical view by invoking the *Next Generation's* Lt. Cmdr. Geordi La Forge and the way that he sees the world.

ANALYTIC PHILOSOPHY AND HOW
GEORDI LA FORGE SEES THE WORLD

Analytic philosophers hold that humans inherently see the world through bias. Put differently, we don't see the world as it is. Instead, we rather arbitrarily categorize objects and the world around us in a way that obscures its actual being. Analytic philosophers, broadly speaking, have committed themselves to identifying the world analytically—i.e., as it is, as opposed to synthetically (combining analytical elements).[19]

The broadcast iterations of the Star Trek franchise indicate that the biases through which we see the world are not biases at all, but the (normative) reasons of the Hegelian Absolute. Hence, to be sentient is to live normatively and we all see the world through similar normative lenses because of the Absolute.[20] This is evident in Star Trek through the way Geordi La Forge (who sees with the aid of a prosthetic device [see Figure 1.1]) comprehends the world around him.

Lt. Cmdr. Geordi La Forge is the Chief Engineer for the Enterprise in the *Next Generation* television series. La Forge was born blind, but he sees with aid of a prosthetic device that allows him to see "much of the EM spectrum ranging from simple heat and infrared through radio waves."[21] During the episode "Heart of Glory" (1988—*Next Generation*) the audience and the Enterprise crew are shown how La Forge actually sees the world (see Figures 1.2, 1.3, and 1.4). Picard describes what La Forge sees as "an undefined form, standing in a visual frenzy." He asks La Forge: "Can you filter out the extraneous information?" La Forge: "No, I get it all simultaneously." Picard: "But it's just a jumble."

PICARD: How can you make head or tail of it?

LA FORGE: I select what I want and then disregard the rest.

La Forge, like the rest of us, knows what to focus on to make sense of the physical world. It's an intuitive process. Thus, like for La Forge, the world is

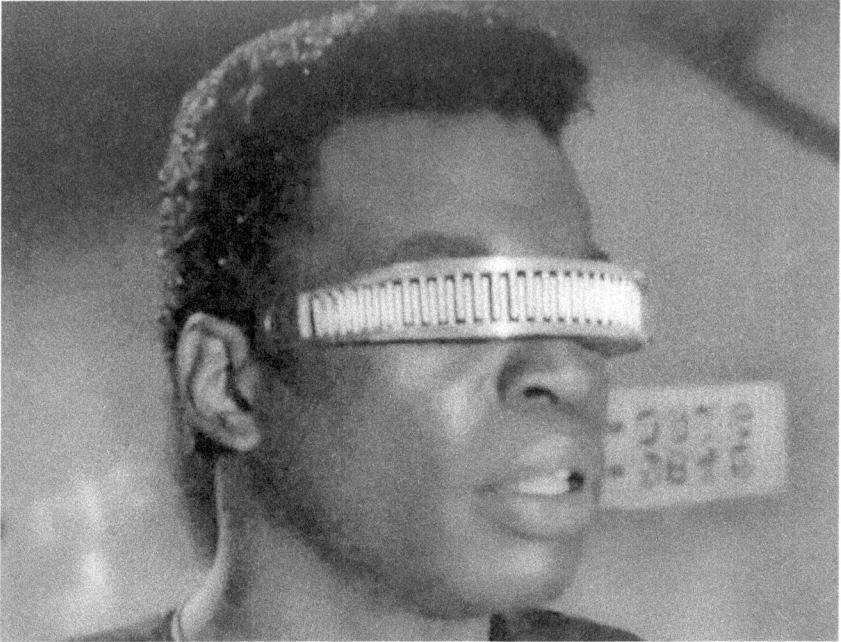

Figure 1.1.　Lt. Cmdr. Geordi La Forge

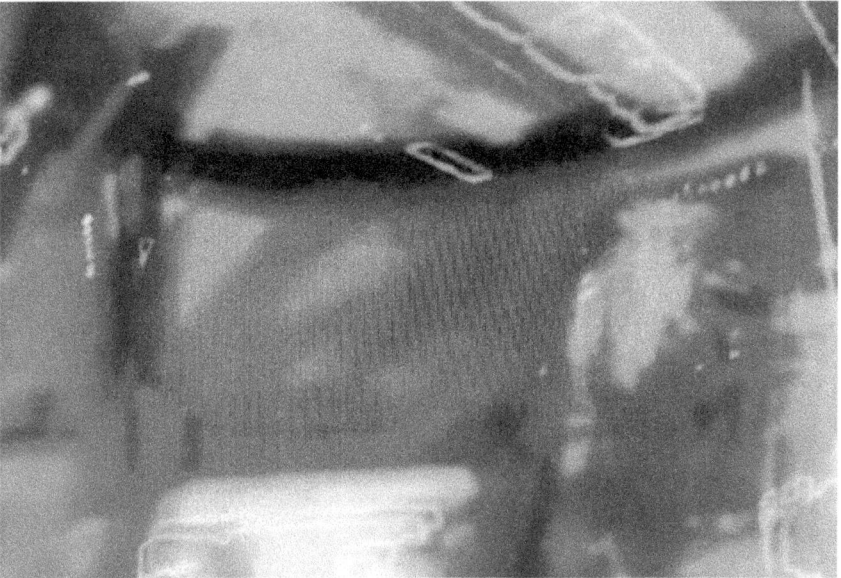

Figure 1.2.　Seeing the World Through La Forge's eyes

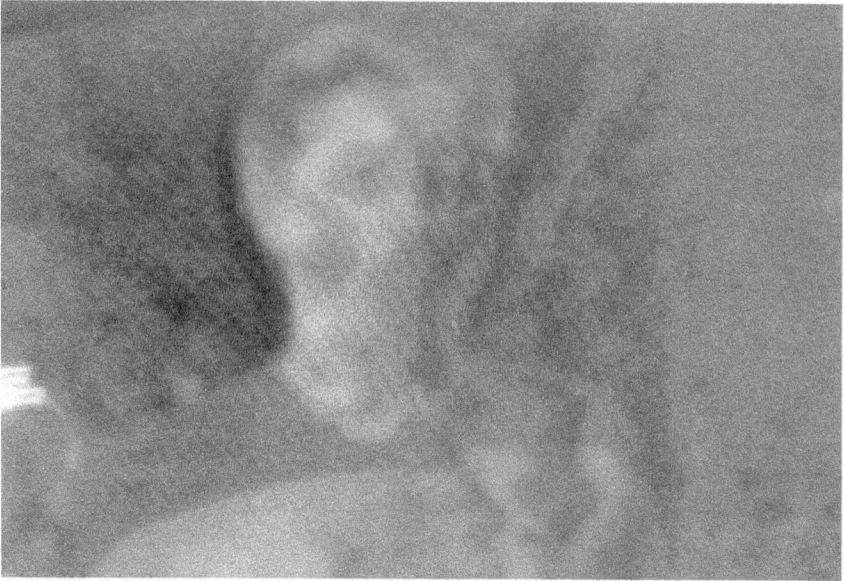

Figure 1.3.   La Forge Looking at Cmdr. Riker

Figure 1.4.   La Forge Looking at Lt. Cmdr. Data

a jumble of light and forms for those of us that have sight, but, yet, we know how to identify a chair, a tree, or another person (for example). Just like La Forge we "select" what we want and "then disregard the rest." La Forge, in another episode, indicates that his vision is limited insofar as it prevents him from seeing as well (normatively) as those that have regular sight: "I want to see in shallow, dim, beautiful human ways. . . . It's not fair . . . I've never seen a rainbow, sunset, sunrise."[22]

CONCLUSION

To bring this discussion back to deconstruction and literary criticism, everyone, more or less, sees in art the same reasons of the world and normative values—as reflected in the way that Geordi La forge perceives reality. The role of the critic is then to sharpen the audience's understanding of these reasons and values—that is, to bring them into greater relief. Hence, the literary critic should not "misread," "problematize," or impute biases that don't actually exist in the art/text. These are the tacks of the deconstructionist.

While particular cases of deconstructionism may, or may not, go too far in taking apart a text, certainly there is a value in adopting a captious attitude toward art/texts—being ever vigilant against racism, sexism, and the like. I would submit that such concerns are largely misplaced. This is because art cannot be manipulated to convey just any agenda—art is only reflective of the Absolute. This is evident with the case of Nazi-era cinema and treated in the next chapter.

NOTES

1. Rita Felski, *The Limits of Critique* (Chicago: The University of Chicago Press, 2015).
2. Marc Redfield, *Theory at Yale: The Strange Case of Deconstruction in America* (New York: Fordham University Press, 2016), 5.
3. Simon Critchley, *The Ethics of Deconstruction: Derrida and Levinas*, 3rd ed. (Edinburgh: Edinburgh University Press, 2014).
4. Redfield, *Theory at Yale*, 5.
5. Timothy W. Luke, *Shows of Force: Power, Politics, and Ideology in Art Exhibitions* (Durham: Duke University Press, 1992), chaps. 1–7.
6. William G. Robbins, *Colony and Empire: The Capitalist Transformation of the American West* (Lawrence: University Press of Kansas, 1994).
7. Luke, *Shows of Force*, 4.
8. Karl Marx, *Karl Marx on Colonialism and Modernization*, Shlomo Avineri, ed. (Garden City, NY: Doubleday, 1968); Harry Harootunian, *Marx After Marx: History*

and Time in the Expansion of Capitalism (New York: Columbia University Press, 2015).

9. Vincenzo Ferrone, *The Enlightenment: History of an Idea* (Princeton: Princeton University Press, 2015); John Robertson, *Enlightenment: A Very Short Introduction* (New York: Oxford University Press, 2015).

10. Ellis, *Against Deconstruction.*

11. Daniel Bernardi, *Star Trek and History: Race-ing Toward a White Future* (Newark: Rutgers University Press, 1998).

12. Ibid., 134.

13. Ibid., 116.

14. Ibid., 127.

15. Ibid., 136.

16. Ibid., 123.

17. George A. Gonzalez, *The Politics of Star Trek* (New York: Palgrave Macmillan, 2015), 120.

18. Ibid., 123.

19. Richard Hanley, *The Metaphysics of Star Trek* (New York: Basic, 1997); Hans-Johann Glock, *What is Analytic Philosophy?* (New York: Cambridge University Press, 2008); Stephen P. Schwartz, *A Brief History of Analytic Philosophy: From Russell to Rawls* (West Sussex, UK: Wiley-Blackwell, 2012); Donovan Wishon and Bernard Linsky, eds., *Acquaintance, Knowledge, and Logic: New Essays on Bertrand Russell's "The Problems of Philosophy"* (Sanford, CA: CSLI Publications, 2015).

20. Donald Phillip Verene, *Hegel's Absolute: An Introduction to Reading the Phenomenology of Spirit* (Albany: State University New York Press, 2007); Stephen Houlgate, *Hegel's 'Phenomenology of Spirit': A Reader's Guide* (New York: Bloomsbury Academic, 2013); James Kreines, *Reason in the World: Hegel's Metaphysics and its Philosophical Appeal* (New York: Oxford University Press, 2015); Andrew Feenberg, *Technosystem: The Social Life of Reason* (Cambridge, MA: Harvard University Press, 2017).

21. *Next Generation*—"Encounter at Farpoint," 1987.

22. *Next Generation*—"The Naked Now," 1987.

Chapter Two

The Absolute and Nazi Cinema

The Nazi government is seemingly the most hateful regime in all of human history. As part of its hate project, the Nazis sought to deploy the modern means of communication to rally the Germany public to its skewed, myopic thinking/agenda.[1] Hitler, in *Mein Kempf*, expressed the view that one factor that led to Germany's defeat in World War I was that the Kaiser's government did a poor job on the propaganda front. Hitler was determined not to let that happen again. Goebbels, in charge of the Nazi Ministry of Propaganda, tried to use the cinema, in particular, as an instrument of political influence and control. As such, Goebbels took personal charge of the movie industry and wanted the making of pro-Nazi movies. Importantly, Goebbels did not want "propaganda movies," which would only appeal to the already convinced. He wanted to naturalize (so to speak) Nazi values by embedding them in artistically appealing movies that would persuade the uninitiated.

Goebbels and the Nazis failed in their effort to make movies that unambiguously forwarded their political agenda.[2] Why? Because art, as reflective of the Hegelian Absolute, is autonomous, and not subject to the kind of instrumental control that Goebbels and the Nazis sought. (I use the Star Trek franchise to outline the values inherent in the Absolute.) Hegel would presumably consider the Nazi project a bad infinity—something at odds with the values of the Absolute—and this is why the Nazis never made a fictional movie that unambiguously conveyed their values and goals. In the end, the Nazis made relatively few political films, and the ones that clearly aligned with the regime's political goals were not Nazi at all. Even the most notorious of Nazi fictional films, *Jud Süs*, cannot in fact be deemed anti-Semitic.

The Politics of Nazi Feature Films

I'll begin my treatment of Nazi films with *Jud Süs*, again the most controversial and detested of all Nazi films. The reason this movie is understandably reviled has more to do with the fact we believe that the portrayal of Jews in this movie is consonant with the vile rhetoric that Hitler et al. directed at the Jews. Moreover, the movie can be justly viewed as a prologue to the Holocaust itself. If *Jud Süs*, however, were made in 1920 instead of 1940, we'd have a different view of it.

Certainly, *Jud Süs* has a Jewish villain—Süss Oppenheimer. But does this make it anti-Semitic? No more than having a German as a villain make a movie anti-German. Many German films did have German villains during the Nazi period. Even having a Jewish villain undercuts (to a certain extent) Nazi anti-Jewish propaganda. Süss Oppenheimer is portrayed as intelligent, capable, and charming in turns. Presumably, virtually any artistically effective protagonist must be cast in this manner. If someone is intelligent, capable and charming, aren't they by definition reformable?

Importantly, *Jud Süs* is set in 1733 and makes the point that Jews at the time were banned from a number of German cities. Presumably, the Nazis applaud this historical fact because it suggested that the German populace has always hated Jews. An honest observer, however, would take away a different point altogether—that Jews have historically suffered terrible, completely unjust discrimination. A viewer might even conclude that Süss Oppenheimer's villainous actions are the result of such unfair treatment meted out to Jews. Additionally, while Oppenheimer plots against the well-being of the people of Swabia through his influence over the Duke of Württemberg, he is not entirely self-interested, as he convinces the Duke to allow Jews to enter the city of Stuttgart. The Jews are cast as very poor and downtrodden (to the Nazi they appear as vermin). A non-bigoted person would see humans who are in great need.

In addition to disastrously raising taxes and overthrowing the democratically elected government council, Süss Oppenheimer forces himself on a virtuous, married woman, who as a result commits suicide. For this heinous act Oppenheimer is executed. Before he is sentenced to death, Oppenheimer cravenly begs for his life. Regardless of how abjectly Oppenheimer begs for his life, in expressing love for his life the viewer can see that Oppenheimer is very human. Oppenheimer's execution can be viewed as politically motivated, as he did not in fact kill anyone, but indirectly (without intending to do so) caused someone's death.

One can certainly see in *Jud Süs* Nazi hate toward Jews (in the end all Jews are again banned from Stuttgart). But if one views this movie absent any foreknowledge of the Nazis or the fact that they were behind *Jud Süs*, one would see a movie where a Jewish man does some very bad things, possibly in response to the terrible discrimination suffered by Jews. Moreover, one would become aware of the very poor conditions that Jews were historically forced to suffer. Thus, I can say with some justification that viewers of *Jud Süs* in the early 1940s were not indoctrinated into anti-Semitism because of it (*Jud Süs* was popular in German-controlled Europe), nor can this movie be viewed as a causal factor behind the Holocaust itself.

If the Nazis were unable to offer a clear-cut vilification of Jews, it's not due to a lack of desire on their part. A truly artistic film, however, seemingly cannot lend itself to the hate and demeaning of an entire people that the Nazis hoped to achieve. Presumably, this was a key factor in explaining why the Nazis made very few explicitly anti-Jewish films. Other than *Jud Süs*, the only other cinematic movie clearly intended to vilify Jews was *Die Rothchilds Aktien auf Waterloo*.[3] This movie is even further off the mark than *Jud Süs*.

In *Die Rothchilds Aktien auf Waterloo* (1940), Nathan Rothchilds (a Jew) plots and schemes to profit from the British war effort against Napoleon in the early 19th century. Significantly, Rothchilds is far from the only London-based financier seeking to profit from the British military campaign—as Rothchilds competes against other British money men who are also speculating on events surrounding the continental war. Even the Duke of Wellington himself is depicted as stealing from funds allocated to the anti-Napoleon coalition. Rothchilds, along with other British financial and military elites, places profit-making over the well-being of the British troops and the overall war effort. Rothschilds's British financier associates treat him badly precisely because he is Jewish, which creates goodwill for Rothschilds among moviegoers. Ian Garden, who compiled an invaluable encyclopedic volume on Nazi political cinema and television, notes the irony that "the unreasonable attitude of the English bankers towards Rothchilds, simply because he is a Jew, actually evokes a certain sympathy and admiration from the viewer for his perseverance in the face of such adversity."[4]

Therefore, in *Die Rothchilds Aktien auf Waterloo* Goebbels et al. are more successful in vilifying the profit motive than anything else. A similar conclusion can be drawn from the Nazi movie *Titanic* (1943), seemingly intended to create anti-British feelings. The movie focuses on the idea that the chief executive of the firm that owned the *Titanic* urged the captain to speed across the North Atlantic, thereby causing its tragic collision with an iceberg. A record-setting voyage would have presumably raised the British company's stock, which the executive had purposively depressed to reap the rewards of the *Titanic*'s triumphant, record-setting Atlantic crossing. The first-class passengers on the ship are cast in a negative light, while the lower-class passengers are sympathetically treated by the filmmakers. Interestingly, James

Cameron's very popular *Titanic* (1995) replicated all of these themes. In the end, the German version of *Titanic* denounces the fact that the chief executive (who made it onto a lifeboat) is exonerated by the British justice system of all wrongdoing in the sinking of *Titanic*. The implication being that wealth and power corrupted the legal proceedings.

A viewer of the movie may have a dimmer view of the British legal system from watching *Titanic*. Nevertheless, the idea that the profit motive places wealth creation above the public good and can cause disaster and that the wealthy have privileged access to the justice system are critiques that can ostensibly be applied to Germany in the 1940s.

This raises the seeming fact that bias in art is not found in what is depicted (as art ostensibly always demands a semblance of balance and intelligible [even reasonable] motives), but in what is not depicted. Thus, what is undoubtedly anti-Semitic about German media (including cinema) under the Nazis is not necessarily movies like *Jud Süs* or *Die Rothchilds Aktien auf Waterloo* but ignoring the horrific conditions that Jews endured under the Nazis. In blacking out the Holocaust (for instance) as it was happening, the public is never offered an opportunity to judge the justice or injustice of this genocide.

The Nazis came to realize that including certain motifs in their cinema could have negative political, even military, implications for them. Four German movies during the Nazi period stand out for their treatment of imperialism: *Der Fuchs von Glenarvon* (1940); *Das Herz der Königin* (1940); *Mein Leben für Irland* (1941); and *Ohm Krüger* (1941). All were directed against the British. Nevertheless, in critically treating British imperialism in East Africa, Ireland, and South Africa, the Nazis artistically cast colonialism as implicitly predicated upon duplicity, bigotry, and violence/death/murder.[5] These movies (particularly the ones set in Ireland) were actually reported by Nazi authorities to have strengthened resistence movements in German-occupied areas.[6]

Another Nazi movie that ironically reflects badly on Nazi rule is *Heimkehr* (1941), which demonizes the treatment that German-speaking minorities putatively received in Eastern Europe prior to World War II. (The movie is set in Poland). The mistreatment of national minorities quickly invokes Nazi treatment of minorities in Germany and its occupied territories.[7]

What is perhaps most philosophically significant about cinema under the Nazis is the kind of political movies they avoided. Upon the Nazi revolution three movies expressly celebrated the Nazi party, the SA, and Hitler himself. Goebbels resisted these movies—even temporarily blocking one from release. Throughout his tenure as the chief of Nazi movies, Goebbels opposed films that explicitly lauded and glorified the Nazi party and Hitler. Such hoary propaganda would convince no one and over time could even grate on rank-and-file Nazis.

This raises two key philosophical questions. First, why is something propaganda and not art? Second, it strongly indicates that, contrary to the theorizing of Richard Rorty, concepts of justice are not malleable or instrumental.

Art is not art when it defines justice in a skewed, self-serving, corrupt manner. Therefore, viewers differentiate "art that is political" (i.e., propaganda) from "political art"—art that provides insight into politics and political phenomena.[8] Movies that would have sought to justify the Nazi party and Hitler—Goebbels thought—would be ineffectual in conveying Nazi political values and convincing viewers of the justice of Nazi political goals.[9] Instead, Goebbels sought to place Germany's putative enemies into roles perpetrating injustice, thereby seeking to explain to viewers that they need protection from the likes of British capitalists and Jewish predators. Another evident political theme in Nazi movies is that Germans can only find justice on German soil, under the protection of the German state.[10]

Significantly, only 10 percent of the 1,300 feature films made under the Nazis can be deemed political in content,[11] and only a limited number can be said to be clearly political tracts.[12] The fact that such a relatively small number of political movies was made under the Nazis is a testament to the inherent difficulty of adapting Nazi values and politics into satisfying art. This is especially the case because Hitler, Goebbels, and the Nazis were determined to indoctrinate the populace.[13] In the end, Goebbels and the Nazis found it easier and more politically valuable to deliver entertainment movies (comedies, adventures, suspense thrillers, etc.) to help the German public escape the drudgeries of wartime production, chronic shortages, and the bad news from the war front.

Nazi Cinema and Intersubjective Agreement

This leads us to Richard Rorty and his notion of *intersubjective agreement*. Rorty, writing in the early 1980s, in fashioning *neopragmatism*, argues that societies are based on *intersubjective agreement*.[14] Thus, what is required for societal stability is enough consensus on a set of ideas—any set of ideas. Hence, what matters is consensus, and not the ideas themselves. Presumably, when there is not enough intersubjective consensus/agreement, then social/political breakdown occurs.

Over ten years before Rorty published his pathbreaking notion of *intersubjective agreement*, *Star Trek*, the original series, episode "Mirror, Mirror" (1967) aired.[15] Members of the Enterprise crew (including Kirk and McCoy), through a technical glitch, are beamed to an alternate universe. The Enterprise (including Spock) exists in this alternate universe, but instead of the Federation the political authority is the "Empire"—where "behavior and discipline" are "brutal, savage." Captain Kirk (from the Federation) refuses to carry out the order to destroy a planet that refuses to comply with the Empire. Spock (sporting a mustache and goatee) notes to Kirk: "No one will question the assassination of a captain who has disobeyed prime orders of the Empire." Kirk: "I command an Enterprise where officers apparently employ private henchmen among the crew, where assassination of superiors is a common means of advancing in rank." McCoy asks "What kind of people are we in this universe?":

> Kirk: Let's find out.
>
> Kirk (to the ship's computer): Read out official record of current command.
>
> Computer: Captain James T. Kirk succeeded to command I.S.S. Enterprise through assassination of Captain Christopher Pike. First action—suppression of Gorlan uprising through destruction of rebel home planet. Second action—execution of 5,000 colonists on Vega 9. . . .
>
> Kirk (interrupting the computer): Cancel
>
> McCoy: Now we know.

Captain Jonathan Archer (*Star Trek: Enterprise* [2001–2005]) from the alternative universe declares that "Great men are not peacemakers. Great men are conquerors" ("In a Mirror, Darkly" 2005). The implication of "Mirror, Mirror" (and "In a Mirror, Darkly") is irrespective of their value system—whether "Empire" or "Federation"—humans can create and lead a vast inter-stellar political formation. Technological progress and political stability would essentially be the same.

The *intersubjective agreement* argument in "Mirror, Mirror" is brought into sharper relief in *Deep Space Nine*, where the alternate universe is revisited a century later.[16] We learn that Kirk's time in the alternate universe had a profound impact. "On my side, Kirk is one of the most famous names in our history." In "Mirror, Mirror" Kirk apprised Spock of a weapon ("the Tantalus field"). From one's quarters a person could zero in on victims and with the push of a button make them disappear. This presages U.S. drone technology, where operators in an air-conditioned facility in Nevada guide small airplanes (drones) flying over regions of the world, and with the push of a button fire missiles on unsuspecting individuals from 50,000 feet.[17] Kirk counseled Spock to use such technology to profoundly change the Empire, and base it on the values of the Federation. When Spock, however, disrupts the *intersubjective agreement* that was the basis of the Empire, it collapses:

Almost a century ago, a Terran starship Captain named James Kirk accidentally exchanged places with his counterpart from your side due to a transporter
accident. Our Terrans were barbarians then, but their Empire was strong.
While your Kirk was on this side, he met a Vulcan named Spock and somehow had a profound influence on him. Afterwards, Spock rose to commander
in chief of the Empire by preaching reforms, disarmament, peace. It was a
remarkable turnabout for his people. Unfortunately for them, when Spock
had completed all these reforms, his empire was no longer in any position to
defend itself against us.

The end result is that the Earth is conquered and occupied.

The Nazi experience indicates that Rorty as well as "Mirror, Mirror" and
"In a Mirror, Darkly" are incorrect that people's political values are inherently malleable. Thus, what we see is that far from exalting the Holocaust
(the logical culmination of Nazi leaders' anti-Jewish screeds), the Hitler
regime hid it from the German public. In the important realm of cinema—
where in the 1930s and 1940s complex political ideas were artistically communicated—the Nazis found it impossible to unambiguously propound their
anti-Jewish biases. Moreover, even the Nazis leaders themselves thought it
futile to produce films that equated the Nazi party and Hitler with justice.
Therefore, the Nazis found the opposite of Rorty's *intersubjective agreement*
notion. Meaningful, popular concepts of justice cannot be concocted out of
whole cloth, and (by implication) neither can political legitimacy.

Then what accounts for the rise of the Nazi regime, a government that
railed against democracy and officially embraced a theory of racial superiority and bigotry? The actual popularity of Nazi ideology among the German
public is something that can never be entirely empirically determined. Nevertheless, judging by Nazi cinema, the authoritarianism and hate of the Hitler
regime were never very popular. Hence, the reticence of Goebbels et al. to
cinematically put these values before the viewing public. Why? To answer
this question, we must turn to the Absolute.

ART AND THE ABSOLUTE

How can we know the *Absolute*?—through art.[18] The *absolute*, identified by
philosopher Georg Hegel,[19] is the driving force behind history.[20] Classicist
Henry Paolucci explains that "art" (along with religion and philosophy) "are
in the end, for Hegel, 'moments' of *absolute spirit*."[21] Similarly, philosopher
William Desmond, in *A Study of Hegel's Aesthetics: Art and the Absolute*,
notes that "Art has an *absolute* dimension; indeed, it belongs together with

religion and philosophy itself as one of the three highest modes of human meaning."[22] If art is among the highest modes of human meaning reflecting the Absolute, would-be art outside of the ideas inherent to the Absolute is not art at all—and perhaps worst of all, may be nothing more than base propaganda.

Why is art empirical documentation of the *absolute*?[23] Humans speculate about the absolute—i.e., that which moves history forward and allows people to lead authentic lives. Precisely because the *absolute* is that which is and which isn't,[24] art/imagination allows for the *absolute* to be conveyed in an intellectually and emotionally satisfying matter.[25] (Notably, the first known philosophy in the Western world [Plato's *Dialogues*] was written in the form of narrative art.) Art, therefore, can supersede philosophy, with the latter serving to dissect/amplify what is accessed/depicted through the former.

Philosophy Professor Jack Kaminsky, drawing explicitly on Hegel's theory of aesthetics, explains that "the artist tries to show men what kind of man would be the fullest expression of the Idea" (i.e., the Absolute).[26] Given the history of Nazi cinema, it can reasonably be argued that Nazi ideation was not an expression of the Absolute.

What qualifies as art? In other words, what counts as an expression of the Absolute? To answer this question I draw on the broadcast iterations of the hugely popular Star Trek franchise. According to Star Trek, the Absolute operates as a progressive dialectic. The progressive dialectic was first specifically identified by Karl Marx.

THE ABSOLUTE IN STAR TREK

Star Trek makes the explicit argument that the *absolute* is indivisible and outside of science. It does so in the *Voyager* episode "Sacred Ground" (1996). In this episode a direct reference to the existence of "spirits" is made—a term Hegel himself would use to denote something beyond material existence (e.g., the physical laws [spirits] of gravity, conservation, thermal dynamics; also, the spirits of love, morality, happiness, etc.). During the episode, the following is said to Janeway: "Mathematics. I can see why you enjoyed it. Solve a problem, get an answer. The answer's either right or wrong. It's very *absolute*." A veiled reference to Hegel's philosophy? Indicative of Hegelian reasoning, the following point is made: "Real is such a relative term." Janeway's materialist (i.e., analytic philosophy) thinking is described in the following: "That would be nice and quantifiable for you, wouldn't it? If the spirits were something you could see and touch and scan with your little devices." Overtly critiquing Kantian rationalism,[27] the following is said to Janeway: "There you go again, always looking for a rational explanation. Well, there isn't one."

The action of "Sacred Ground" centers on the fact that Voyager crew member, Kes, becomes incapacitated when she comes into contact with an "energy field." Voyager's doctor is unable to bring Kes out of her coma, and she's on the verge of death. Unable to find a scientific explanation for the field or Kes's condition, Captain Janeway is forced to appeal to the "monks" that oversee the energy field. They consider it a manifestation of their deities—the *Ancestral Spirits*. In order to save Kes, Janeway is told "that the only thing that matters is finding your connection to the spirits." In the end, it is only when Janeway accepts that something beyond material reality exists (i.e., the *Ancestral Spirits*) that Kes is revived.

Therefore, rationality in Star Trek, as for Hegel, is found not in reducing the absolute to an object (subject to scientific analysis and manipulation), but in understanding the ontology of the absolute. Following from Star Trek, the absolute functions as a *progressive dialectic*—moving humanity toward a classless society, free of gender and ethnic biases.[28] As conveyed in Star Trek, human agency plays a prime role in this meta-narrative.

THE PROGRESSIVE DIALECTIC OF STAR TREK

The *progressive dialectic* was initially identified by Karl Marx, and later acted upon by Leon Trotsky. The progressive dialectic is artistically represented in the "United Federation of Planets"—the fictional interstellar political entity in Star Trek that humans lead. The failure to speculate about the *absolute* and pursue the *progressive dialectic* is to precipitate disaster for humanity. Star Trek in artistically conveying the progressive dialectic makes the specific argument that if humanity/civilization is to survive/thrive that capitalist values have to be abandoned and neoliberalism has to be replaced.

STAR TREK AND CAPITALISM

Star Trek explicitly rejects capitalism in the *Next Generation* episode "The Neutral Zone" (1988). A wealthy businessman, named "Ralph Offenhouse," from the late-20th century is revived from a cryogenic chamber floating in space. (*Next Generation* takes place in the 24th century.) Upon being awoken, Ralph explains that "I have a substantial portfolio. It's critical I check on it." Later, he adds "I have to phone Geneva right away about my accounts. The interest alone could be enough to buy even this ship." Ralph dons an attitude of arrogance, entitlement, and authority. He tells Captain Picard "I demand you see me." When Picard tries to put Ralph off by referring to the sensitive situation the ship is dealing with at the time, Ralph retorts "I'm sure that whatever it is seems very important to you. My situation is far more critical." Ralph condescends to the Captain: "It is simply that I have more to protect than a man in your position could possibly imagine. No offense, but a military career has never been considered upwardly mobile." Picard, losing his patience, informs Ralph that his value system (and attitude) is misplaced and disdained in the current epoch:

Picard: A lot has changed in three hundred years. People are no longer obsessed with the accumulation of "things." We have eliminated hunger, want, the need for possessions. We have grown out of our infancy.

Ralph: You've got it wrong. It's never been about "possessions"—it's about power.[29]

Picard: Power to do what?

Ralph: To control your life, your destiny.

Picard: That kind of control is an illusion.

Chastened, Ralph asks "There's no trace of my money—my office is gone—what will I do? How will I live?" Picard explains "Those material needs no longer exist." Ralph, invoking the values of the late 20th century, responds by asking: "Then what's the challenge?" Picard, seemingly outlining the values of 24th-century Earth, retorts: "To improve yourself . . . enrich yourself. Enjoy it, Mister Offenhouse."

Similarly, in the *Deep Space Nine* episode "In the Cards" (1997), Jake Sisko exclaims "I'm Human, I don't have any money." Nog, a Ferengi—an alien race that operates on the profit-motive—is critical of 24th-century humanity: "It's not my fault that your species decided to abandon currency-based economics in favor of some philosophy of self-enhancement." Shifting humanity's (America's) values away from "currency-based economics" and toward a "philosophy of self-enhancement" mirrors Karl Marx's point that in moving from capitalism to communism society would go "from each according to his ability, to each according to his needs!"—i.e., communist politics would focus on "the all-around development of the individual."[30] Or as Jake told Nog: "There's nothing wrong with our philosophy. We work to better ourselves and the rest of Humanity."

Indicative of how humans in the 24th century have undergone a profound paradigm shift in values and outlook, Quark, a Ferengi who traveled back to mid-20th-century Earth (more specifically, the United States), concludes from his dealings with humans (Americans) in this epoch, that "these humans, they're not like the ones from the [24th-century] Federation. They're crude, gullible, and greedy."[31] Marx offers a consonant rebuke of the cultural/social ethos of capitalists: "Contempt for theory, art, history, and for man as an end in himself . . . is the real, conscious standpoint, the virtue of the man of money."[32]

Therefore, Star Trek takes the Enlightenment to its logical conclusion—namely, that modernity, science, and reason can serve as the basis for a peaceful, highly productive, and thriving world.[33] Star Trek is optimistic insofar as arguing that as global society accepts modernity, reason, and science (i.e., the progressive dialectic), humans will collectively achieve a higher plane of intelligence, knowledge, and emotional maturity. (An optimism shared by Marx: in "communist society . . . the all-round development of the individual" will be achieved.[34]) This higher plane of existence, however, requires the overthrow of the neoliberal order.

NEOLIBERALISM

To the American Revolutionary War (see below), the U.S. Civil War (see below), and the American fight against fascism (original series—"City on the Edge of Forever" 1967), Star Trek adds to America's revolutionary "moments" with the Bell Uprising. Aired in 1995, "Past Tense" is centered on this fictional uprising. The characters Sisko, Bashir, and Dax are accidentally sent back to 2024 San Francisco, where, as in "City on the Edge of Forever," they alter Earth's history for the worse. Upon being beamed to the past, Sisko and Bashir are separated from Dax. Without any identification (or money) Sisko and Bashir are forcibly interned in an urban detainment camp for the poor and dispossessed. It is described in script notes as follows:

> Sisko and Bashir ENTER a street lined by dirty, dilapidated buildings, with boarded up windows and impromptu campsites set up in the doorways and stairwells. It's a sharp contrast to the relatively clean city outside. The street is crowded with poorly dressed homeless men, women, and children, of all ages and races, many standing in a long food line.[35]

Sisko, who is knowledgeable about 21st-century Earth, explains that "by the early twenty-twenties there was a place like this in every major city in the United States."

Bashir asks: Why are these people in here? Are they criminals?

Sisko: No. People with criminal records weren't allowed in the Sanctuary Districts.

Bashir: Then what did they do to deserve this?

Sisko: Nothing. They're just people. People without jobs or places to live.

Bashir: So they get put in here?

Sisko: Welcome to the twenty-first century.

Writing in the mid-1990s about internment camps for the poor and home-less being in place in every major American city within 30 years is an explicit critique of the neoliberal project, which was well established by the 1990s.[36] Neoliberalism, whose proponents prioritize the free movement of capital, goods, and services, has been devastating to numerous U.S. urban centers, particularly in the former industrial American heartland.[37] Cities like Detroit[38] and Cleveland[39]—which were global centers of industrial production—have been hollowed out as the U.S. manufacturing base has been shifted to cheap-wage venues in the U.S. South, Mexico, and China.[40] One of the displaced residents of the San Francisco Sanctuary District explains that "I used to be a Plant Manager at ChemTech Industries." The result has been pronounced urban decay in once wealthy and prosperous cities,[41] where a substantial homeless population is an enduring phenomenon.[42]

Moreover, the Great Recession of 2008 has caused persistently high unem-ployment.[43] A historically destabilizing factor of capitalism is the tendency of capital equipment (i.e., technology) to replace labor.[44] In a 2012 op-ed piece in the *New York Times*, Princeton economist Paul Krugman holds "there's no question that in some high-profile industries, technology is displacing work-ers of all, or almost all, kinds."[45] A Sanctuary District resident explains that "I came to San Francisco to work in a brewery but they laid a bunch of us off when they got some new equipment and so I ended up here." Another of the characters in "Past Tense" notes that "right now jobs are hard to come by . . . what with the economy and all." The former plant manager plaintively explains: "Most of us agreed to live here [in the San Francisco Sanctuary District] because they promised us jobs. I don't know about you, but I haven't been on any job interviews lately. And neither has anyone else. They've for-gotten about us."

The overriding need to pursue societal justice (i.e., topple neoliberalism/ capitalism) is made clear in "Past Tense." While in the Sanctuary District (in 2024 San Francisco), Sisko intervenes in a fight, which accidentally results in the death of one Gabriel Bell—the would-be leader of the Bell Uprising. Like the victory of the Nazis in World War II ("City on the Edge of Forever"), this erases the entire history of the Federation. Meanwhile, back in the 24th century, all that remains of the original time line is the ship (the Defiant) that beamed Sisko, Bashir, and Dax to the past. Uncertain when Sisko et al. are located, members of the Defiant crew randomly transport into Earth's past. They conclude Sisko et al. "arrived before the year twenty-forty-eight."

How can you be sure?

Because we were just there. And that wasn't the mid-twenty-first century that I read about in school. It's been changed. *Earth history had its rough patches, but never that rough.*

Therefore, the absence of the Bell Uprising to spark the revolution that would politically challenge the current neoliberalism regime would ostensibly result in Earth's society devolving into some type of nightmare scenario as early as 2048.

The original time line is restored when Sisko takes the name Gabriel Bell and fulfills his role in history. One of the successes of the Bell Uprising was the ability of residents of the Sanctuary District to evade a government blockade of the "Interface" (i.e., the internet—which was a nascent technology when "Past Tense" aired in 1995) and convey their personal stories to the world. One resident explains: "My name is Henry Garcia . . . and I've been living here two years now. . . . I've never been in trouble with the law or anything. . . . I don't want to hurt anybody. . . . I just want a chance to work and live like regular people."

Confirming the interpretation of Star Trek as positing American history as a series of progressive events ("revolutions") is "The Savage Curtain" (1969—original series) and "The Omega Glory" (1968—original series). The episode "The Omega Glory" depicts a world with an identical history to that of Earth's, except in this instance the Cold War resulted in globally devastating nuclear/biological war—where humans were reduced to a veritable Stone Age. Kirk ultimately realizes that the segment of the population that represented the West views the U.S. Constitution as a sacred document. But they cannot read it, so Kirk explains to them: "That which you called Ee'd Ple bnista was not written for chiefs or kings or warriors or the rich and powerful, but for all the people!" Kirk proceeds to read directly from this document (the Ee'd Plebnista), which is the Constitution:

We the people of the United States, in order to form a more perfect union, establish justice, ensure domestic tranquillity, provide for the common defense, promote the general welfare, and secure the blessings of liberty to ourselves and our posterity . . . do ordain and establish this constitution.

Asserting the revolutionary implications of the American Revolution and the Constitution that followed, Kirk declares "these words and the words that follow. . . They must apply to everyone or they mean nothing!" Kirk adds "liberty and freedom have to be more than just words."

In "The Savage Curtain" the Enterprise crew meets the incarnation of Abraham Lincoln. While acknowledging that this is not the real Lincoln, Kirk insists that the crew treat him with the respect and deference due this great historical figure—the leader of what many consider to be the second American Revolution (i.e., the victorious Northern Cause in the U.S. Civil War).[46] Kirk notes: "I cannot conceive it possible that Abraham Lincoln . . . could have actually been reincarnated. And yet his kindness, his gentle wisdom, his humor, everything about him is so right." McCoy chides Kirk: "Practically the entire crew has seen you . . . treat this impostor like the real thing . . . when he can't possibly be the real article. Lincoln died three centuries ago hundreds of light-years away." Spock observes to Kirk: "President Lincoln has always been a very personal hero to you." Kirk retorts: "Not only to me." Spock: "Agreed."

Thus, Star Trek is optimistic in that America is evolving toward an ideal, classless society. The American Revolution, the Civil War, and the Bell Uprising (i.e., the defeat of neoliberalism) are necessary stops on this road to (worldwide) utopia. This is reflective of American Marxists' view that U.S. history is an unfolding revolutionary process, the end result of which is the establishment of an ideal socialist/communist society. Sidney Hook, for instance, writing in 1933 (when he was still a follower of the Russian revolutionary Leon Trotsky [i.e., a Trotskyist]) reasoned that "America had gone through her second revolution to break up the semi-feudal slavocracy which barred the expansion of industrial capitalism."[47] Operating in the U.S. since the 1920s, Trotskyists hold that the American Revolution and the Civil War remain incomplete until the worker state is in place.[48] Put differently, these revolutions will be completed by the socialist revolution (the Bell Uprising[?]). (It is noteworthy and significant that in the episode where the Bell Uprising is conveyed, the phrase "Neo-Trotskyists" is used; also, in another episode, a passage from the Communist Manifesto is read.[49])

CONCLUSION: NAZI GERMANY AND THE PROGRESSIVE DIALECTIC

I am relying on the Star Trek franchise to argue that the Absolute ontologically operates as the progressive dialectic, and that the end result of this dialectic is a classless society, free of gender and ethnic biases. Put differently, the conception of justice that emanates from the absolute is one of complete fairness and compassion.

How does this relate to Nazi Germany? Did the absolute and the conception of justice inherent within it not apply to the German public during the Nazi period? Looking at the Nazi party's cinema, the values of the absolute were pertinent and commonsensical in Germany during the 1930s and 1940s. We see this in the fact that the Nazis in their cinema critiqued British imperialism as inherently unjust because it was predicated on bigotry, duplicity, violence, and death. Similarly, we see the Nazis through cinema explicitly critique the idea that it is wrong to victimize people simply because they speak a different language and/or have a different national identity (*Heimkehr*). Moreover, in the German movie *Titanic* class stratification is cast in a negative light—with the first-class passengers portrayed as aloof, whereas those in third class are conveyed as friendly and warm. *Titanic* also specifically articulates the idea that wealth and corporate power subvert justice. *Die Rothchilds Aktien auf Waterloo* and *Titanic* share the motif that the profit motive drives people to (disastrously) disregard the public good for their own self-interest. Therefore, in Nazi cinema, consistent with the progressive dialectic as outlined in the Star Trek franchise, we see sharp critiques of class inequality, the profit motive, and jingoism. Conversely, the Nazi party's values and goals never find firm cinematic footing.

NOTES

1. David Welch, *The Third Reich: Politics and Propaganda*, 2nd ed. (New York: Routledge, 2002); Randall L. Bytwerk, *Bending Spines: The Propagandas of Nazi Germany and the German Democratic Republic* (Lansing: Michigan State University Press, 2004); Aristotle A. Kallis, *Nazi Propaganda and the Second World War* (New York: Palgrave Macmillan, 2008).

2. Eric Rentschler, *The Ministry of Illusion: Nazi Cinema and Its Afterlife* (Cambridge, MA: Harvard University Press, 1996); Linda Schulte-Sasse, *Entertaining the Third Reich: Illusions of Wholeness in Nazi Cinema* (Durham: Duke University Press, 1996).

3. Ian Garden, *The Third Reich's Celluloid War: Propaganda in Nazi Feature Films, Documentaries and Television* (Gloucestershire, UK: History Press, 2015), 72–77.

4. Garden, *The Third Reich's Celluloid War*, 83. My treatment of Nazi films draws mostly from this highly detailed source.

5. Garden, *The Third Reich's Celluloid War*, chap. 3.

6. Garden, *The Third Reich's Celluloid War*, 50.

7. Garden, *The Third Reich's Celluloid War*, 127.

8. Jacques Rancière, *Aesthetics and Its Discontents*, trans. Steve Corcoran (Malden, MA: Polity, 2009).

9. David Welch, *Propaganda and the German Cinema, 1933–1945* (New York: Oxford University Press, 2001), chap. 2.

10. Welch, *Propaganda and the German Cinema, 1933–1945*; Siegfriend Kracauer, *From Caligari to Hitler: A Psychological History of the German Film* (Princeton: Princeton University Press, 2004 [1947]).

11. Garden, *The Third Reich's Celluloid War*, 20; also see Mary-Elizabeth Olsen, *Nazi Cinema as Entertainment: The Politics of Entertainment in the Third Reich* (Rochester, NY: Camden House, 2004).

12. Certain movies are counted as political that were mostly entertainment movies but to some significant extent touched on political ideas. Garden, *The Third Reich's Celluloid War*.

13. Jeffrey Herf, *The Jewish Enemy: Nazi Propaganda during World War II and the Holocaust* (Cambridge, MA: Belknap, 2008); Susan Bachrach and Steven Luckert, *State of Deception: The Power of Nazi Propaganda* (Washington, DC: U.S. Holocaust Memorial Museum, 2009).

14. Richard Rorty, *Philosophy and the Mirror of Nature* (Princeton: Princeton University Press, 1981); Michael Bacon, *Richard Rorty: Pragmatism and Political Liberalism* (Lanham: Lexington Books, 2007); Neil Gross, *Richard Rorty: The Making of an American Philosopher* (Chicago: University of Chicago Press, 2008).

15. George A. Gonzalez, *The Politics of Star Trek: Justice, War, and the Future* (New York: Palgrave Macmillan, 2015).

16. *Deep Space Nine*—"Crossover," 1994.

17. John F. Burns, "U.N. Panel To Assess Drone Use," *New York Times*, Jan. 25, 2013, A4; Lloyd C. Gardner, *Killing Machine: The American Presidency in the Age of Drone Warfare* (New York: New Press, 2013); Thom Shanker, "Simple, Low-Cost Drones a Boost for U.S. Military," *New York Times*, Jan. 25, 2013, A12; Declan Walsh, and Ihsanullan Tipu Mehsud, "Civilian Deaths in Drone Strikes Cited in Report," *New York Times*, Oct. 22, 2013, A1; Christopher Drew and Dave Philipps, "Burnout Forces U.S. to Curtail Drone Flights," *New York Times*, June 17, 2015, A1.

18. William Maker, ed., *Hegel and Aesthetics* (Albany: State University of New York Press, 2000); Kirk Pillow, *Sublime Understanding: Aesthetic Reflection in Kant and Hegel* (Cambridge, MA: MIT Press, 2000).

19. Donald Phillip Verene, *Hegel's Absolute: An Introduction to Reading the Phenomenology of Spirit* (Albany: State University New York Press, 2007); Stephen Houlgate, *Hegel's 'Phenomenology of Spirit': A Reader's Guide* (New York: Bloomsbury Academic, 2013); Brady Bowman, *Hegel and the Metaphysics of Absolute Negativity* (Cambridge: Cambridge University Press, 2015).

20. Robert L. Perkins, ed., *History and System: Hegel's Philosophy of History* (Albany: State University of New York, 1984); Will Dudley, ed., *Hegel and History* (Albany: State University of New York Press, 2009).

21. Henry Paolucci, "Introduction" in *Hegel: On the Arts*, Henry Paolucci, ed., 2nd ed. (Smyrna, DE: Griffon House, 2001), xix, emphasis added.

22. William Desmond, *Art and the Absolute: A Study of Hegel's Aesthetics* (Albany: State University of New York Press, 1986), xii, emphasis added.

23. Jack Kaminsky, *Hegel on Art: An Interpretation of Hegel's Aesthetics* (Albany: State University of New York Press, 1962).

24. Stephen Mumford, *Metaphysics: A Very Short Introduction* (New York: Oxford University Press, 2012).

25. Jennifer Ann Bates, *Hegel's Theory of Imagination* (Albany: State University of New York Press, 2004); Richard Eldridge, *Beyond Representation: Philosophy and Poetic Imagination* (New York: Cambridge University Press, 2011).

26. Kaminsky, *Hegel on Art*, 29.

27. In the *Critique of Pure Reason*, Kant argues that reason and empiricism can account for all phenomena. Immanuel Kant, *Critique of Pure Reason*, trans. Max Muller (New York: Penguin, 2008 [1781]).

28. Gonzalez, *The Politics of Star Trek*.

29. Sam Polk, a former hedge-fund trader, in a 2014 op-ed piece posited a critical assessment of the ethos that dominates the American finance community: "Wall Street is a toxic culture that encourages the grandiosity of people who are desperately trying to feel powerful." Sam Polk, "For the Love of Money," *New York Times*, Jan. 19, 2014,SR1.

30. Karl Marx, *The Critique of the Gotha Programme* (London: Electric Book Co., 2001 [1875]), 20. Web.

31. *Deep Space Nine*—"Little Green Men," 1995.

32. Karl Marx, *On the Jewish Question*. 1844. Web.

33. Tom Rockmore, *Marx's Dream: From Capitalism to Communism* (Chicago: University of Chicago Press, 2018).

34. Marx, *The Critique of the Gotha Programme*, 20.

35. http://www.st-minutiae.com/academy/literature329/457.txt.

36. Gérard Duménil, and Dominique Lévy, *Capital Resurgent: Roots of the Neoliberal Revolution*, trans. Derek Jeffers (Cambridge, MA: Harvard University Press, 2004); Daniel Stedman Jones, *Masters of the Universe: Hayek, Friedman, and the Birth of Neoliberal Politics* (Princeton: Princeton University Press, 2012); Quinn Slobodian, *Globalists: The End of Empire and the Birth of Neoliberalism* (Cambridge, MA: Harvard University Press, 2018).

37. Guin A. McKee, *The Problem of Jobs: Liberalism, Race, and Deindustrialization in Philadelphia* (Chicago: University of Chicago Press, 2009); Timothy Williams,"For Shrinking Cities, Destruction Is a Path to Renewal," *New York Times*, Nov. 12, 2013, A15.

38. Thomas J. Sugrue, *The Origins of the Urban Crisis: Race and Inequality in Postwar Detroit* (Princeton: Princeton University Press, 2005); Joe Drape,"Bankruptcy for Ailing Detroit, but Prosperity for Its Teams," *New York Times*, Oct. 14, 2013, A1.

39. Carol Poh Miller and Robert Wheeler, *Cleveland: A Concise History* (Bloomington: Indiana University Press, 2009).

40. Mary Elizabeth Gallagher, *Contagious Capitalism: Globalization and the Politics of Labor in China* (Princeton: Princeton University Press, 2005); Kelly Sims Gallagher, *China Shifts Gears: Automakers, Oil, Pollution, and Development* (Cambridge, MA: MIT Press, 2006); Louis Uchitelle, "Goodbye, Production (and Maybe Innovation)." *New York Times*, Dec. 24, 2006, sec. 3 p. 4; Peter S. Goodman, " U.S. and Global Economies Slipping in Unison," *New York Times*, August 24, 2008, A1; David Koistinen, *Confronting Decline: The Political Economy of Deindustrialization in Twentieth-Century New England* (Gainesville: University Press of Florida, 2013).

41. Susan M. Wachter and Kimberly A. Zeuli, eds., *Revitalizing American Cities* (Philadelphia: University of Pennsylvania Press, 2013); Monica Davey, "A Picture of Detroit Ruin, Street by Forlorn Street," *New York Times*, Feb. 18., 2014, A1; Jon Hurdle, "Philadelphia Forges Plan To Rebuild From Decay," *New York Times*, Jan. 1, 2014, B1.

42. Deborah K. Padgett, Benjamin F. Henwood, Sam J. Tsemberis, *Housing First: Ending Homelessness, Transforming Systems, and Changing Lives* (New York: Oxford University Press, 2015); Craig Willse, *The Value of Homelessness: Managing Surplus Life in the United States* (Minneapolis: University of Minnesota Press, 2015).

43. Kristin S. Seefedt and John D. Graham, *America's Poor and the Great Recession* (Bloomington: Indiana University Press, 2013); "Ten States Still Have Fewer Jobs Since Recession," Reuters, March 25, 2016; David Leonhardt, "We're Measuring the Economy All Wrong," *New York Times*, September 14, 2018. Web.

44. Claire Cain Miller, "Smarter Robots Move Deeper Into Workplace," *New York Times*, December 16, 2014, A1; Farhad Manjoo, "Uber's Business Model Could Change Your Work," *New York Times*, January 29, 2015, B1; Zeynep Tufekci, "The Machines Are Coming," *New York Times*, April 19, 2015, SR4; Claire Cain Miller, "What's Really Killing Jobs? It's Automation, Not China," *New York Times*, December 22, 2016, A3; Alex Williams, "Robot-Proofing Your Child's Future," *New York Times*, December 14, 2017, D1; Peter S. Goodman, "Sweden Adds Human Touch to a Robotic Future," *New York Times*, December 28, 2017, A1; Liz Alderman, "Humans Wanted, But Robots Work," *New York Times*, April 17, 2018, B1; Niraj Chokshi, "Robot Cures Human Headache: Putting Together Ikea Furniture," *New York Times*, April 19, 2018, B8.

45. Paul Krugman, "Robots and Robber Barons," *New York Times*, Dec. 10, 2012, A27.

46. James M. McPherson, *Abraham Lincoln and the Second American Revolution* (New York: Oxford University Press, 1992); James Oakes, *Freedom National: The Destruction of Slavery in the United States* (New York: W.W. Norton & Company, 2012).

47. Sidney Hook, *Towards the Understanding of Karl Marx* (New York: John Day, 1933), 294–295.

48. James P. Cannon, *The History of American Trotskyism: Report of a Participant* (New York: Pioneer Publishers, 1944); Constance Ashton Myers, *The Prophet's Army: Trotskyists in America, 1928–1941* (Westport, CT: Greenwood Press, 1977); A. Belden Fields, *Trotskyism and Maoism: Theory and Practice in France and the United States* (New York: Praeger, 1988), chap. 4; Bryan D. Palmer, *James P. Cannon and the Origins of the American Revolutionary Left, 1890–1928* (Urbana: University of Illinois Press, 2010); Donna T. Haverty-Stacke, *Trotskyists on Trial: Free Speech and Political Persecution Since the Age of FDR* (New York: New York University Press, 2016).

49. In the midst of a labor strike (*Deep Space Nine*—"Bar Association" 1996), a character reads directly from the *Communist Manifesto*: "Workers of the world, unite. You have nothing to lose but your chains."

Chapter Three

Star Trek, Scientism, the Progressive Dialectic, and the Pre-Theoretical

The pre-theoretical consists of phenomena that science cannot explain, such as creativity, ageing, the survival instinct, the drive to procreate, emotions (such as love and happiness), and laughter/comedy/sarcasm. Analytic philosophy is predicated on the notion that science someday will be able to account for all currently pre-theoretical aspects of the world.[1] Critics label this thinking *scientism*.[2]

The broadcast iterations of Star Trek are set centuries into the future. Perhaps the intuitive appeal of the franchise is precisely the notion that scientism has not prevailed. Namely, regardless of how technologically advanced humans became, the pre-theoretical continued to stand outside of science. Indicative of how the pre-theoretical in Star Trek remained essentially unchanged 400 years into the future, someone from the 20th century explains that in the 24th century life is "the same dance."[3]

The durability of the pre-theoretical in Star Trek is glaringly evident in three factors: 1.) death (i.e., dying of old age), 2.) the human mind, and 3.) the inherent perils of time travel. Perhaps most significant is the *Next Generation* episode "The Masterpiece Society" (1992), which expressly argues that science cannot overcome the pre-theoretical, and, just as importantly, that science itself is a function of the pre-theoretical.

By insisting on the autonomy and indivisibility of the pre-theoretical, Star Trek lends itself to a Hegelian understanding of the world.[4] More specifically, human history is guided by a meta-narrative—i.e., the *absolute*. This meta-narrative is consonant with Karl Marx's *progressive dialectic*—whereby the end point of human history is the classless society, free of gender or ethnic biases.[5] Star Trek's contribution to our understanding of the absolute and the progressive dialectic is the emphasis upon human agency. The Star Trek text, drawing from the lessons of the 20th and 21st centuries, indicates that humanity's decisions with regard to the pre-theoretical (i.e., the absolute and the progressive dialectic) will determine the future of civilization.

THE PRE-THEORETICAL IN STAR TREK:
DEATH, THE HUMAN MIND, AND TIME TRAVEL

In the very first episode of *Next Generation* DeForest Kelley makes a cameo appearance (playing his alter ego Dr. Leonard McCoy from the original series). McCoy is 137 years old. He looks his age. Thus, while humans ostensibly live longer in the 24th century, the ravages of time still afflict them—including death. McCoy states that he is not "troubled" by his elderly state—"What's so damned troubling about not having died?"[6] "Remember Me" (1990—*Next Generation*) begins with a conversation between an elderly man named "Quaice" and Dr. Crusher. Quaice laments the fact that death is taking so many of his family members and longtime friends: "You know what the worst part of growing old is? So many of the people you've known all your life are gone."

Significantly, progress with regard to death in Star Trek is not cast as overcoming it, but in accepting it. Pointing out that "Cryonics"—the practice of freezing the dead in the hope of reviving them later—was "a fad in the late twentieth century," Dr. Crusher explains that "People feared dying. It terrified them." Apparently, in the future this fear would subside: "The process of cryonics was never more than a fad, and did not continue much beyond the mid-twenty first century."[7] In another episode, Picard explains to an alien that: "You see, we are mortal. Our time in this universe is finite. That is one of the truths that all humans must learn."[8]

Like death, the human mind is outside of science in Star Trek. *Voyager*, like the *Next Generation*, is set in the 24th century. The doctor on the starship Voyager makes the point that the "brain is still a somewhat mysterious organ."[9] Doctor Bashir from *Deep Space Nine* (also set in the 24th century) similarly explains that "there's still a great deal about the way the brain operates we don't understand." Bashir adds that "one of my professors at medical school used to say that the brain had a spark of life that can't be replicated."[10] Even the minds of sentient androids cannot be replicated, as when Data's android "daughter" died and she could not be brought back.[11]

The persistence of the pre-theoretical is particularly evident in the issue of time travel. The franchise adopts a temporal prime directive—where incursions into the past are to be avoided for fear that changing the past (however trivially)—can have profound effects on the future. There are two related issues at play here: one, that reality operates dialectically—and consonant with

Hegel's argumentation—everything is connected to everything else.[12] Therefore, contrary to the reasoning underlying analytic philosophy, we cannot isolate the parts of reality from the whole. Reflective of this is the *Voyager* episode "Year of Hell" (1997), where a ship that is able to manipulate past events—despite sophisticated and continuous efforts—could not produce the outcome it desired.

Moreover, the most unpredictable aspect of the time line is probably humans. As Spock wisely notes: "No one can guarantee the actions of another."[13] Put differently, humans' (or sentient beings') responses to events is fundamentally unpredictable (reflective of how the mind is outside of science), and it is precisely this unpredictability that makes altering past events so perilous. This is evident in the *Next Generation* episode "Yesterdays' Enterprise" (1990)—where a Starfleet ship from the past (the Enterprise-C) enters the present, thereby profoundly altering the time line. The result of changing the time line is that the Federation and the Klingons have been engaged in a decades-long war—which the Federation is on the verge of losing. We learn that the ship from the past was trying to help a Klingon outpost that was under attack when it entered the fissure in time that brought it to the future. Picard et al. reason that a Starfleet ship coming to the aid of a Klingon space station could have convinced the Klingons at the time to negotiate a peace treaty, thereby avoiding decades of devastating war. "The Klingons regard honor above all else. If the crew of the Enterprise-C had died fighting for the survival of a Klingon outpost, it would be considered a meaningful act of honor by the Klingon Empire." Therefore, by prematurely exiting the battle by coming to the future the Enterprise-C inadvertently precipitated a war. "One more ship will make no difference in the here and now. But twenty-two years ago, one ship could have stopped this war before it started."

The inherent unpredictability of people's responses to changes in events is at the center of "Tapestry" (1993—*Next Generation*). Captain Picard as a young cadet in Starfleet Academy engaged in a fight that resulted in his being stabbed in the heart, which was then replaced with a mechanical one. Some thirty years later, as Captain of the Enterprise, Picard subsequently dies because of his artificial heart. The omnipotent Q intervenes and allows Picard to relive the events that lead to his stabbing. Picard takes this opportunity and never gets stabbed, nor receives a mechanical heart—allowing him to putatively keep living beyond the accident that later kills him. After Picard avoids getting stabbed, Q returns him to the present, where he finds he is no longer Captain of the Enterprise and determines that he does not like himself now: "I can't live out my days as that person. That man is bereft of passion and imagination. That is not who I am." Q explains to Picard that without coming close to death (with his "Nausicaan" impaling) he remained rather inured to the reality that the opportunities to make a mark are finite:

> The Jean-Luc Picard you wanted to be, the one who did not fight the Nausicaan, had quite a different career from the one you remember. That Picard never had a brush with death, never came face to face with his own mortality, never realized how fragile life is or how important each moment must be. So his life never came into focus. He drifted for much of his career, with no plan or agenda, going from one assignment to the next, never seizing the opportunities that presented themselves. . . . And no one ever offered him a command. He learned to play it safe. And he never, ever got noticed by anyone.

In the end, Picard chooses death over living life as what he perceives as a minimal contributor to society: "I would rather die as the man I was than live the life I just saw."

Next Generation explored the idea of basing a society entirely on the idea of deploying science to circumscribe the pre-theoretical. It does so in the episode "The Masterpiece Society."

"THE MASTERPIECE SOCIETY"

The Enterprise, in "The Masterpiece Society," comes upon an "engineered society." "Our ancestors came from Earth to develop a perfect society. They believed that through controlled procreation, they could create people without flaws and those people would build a paradise." A goal of this society is to overcome the pre-theoretical, specifically the autonomy of the human mind: "I have been bred to fill this specific role. We grow up knowing exactly what our society needs from us. What we are expected to do." Picard takes issue with the principles that guides the society on "Moab Four" and its explicit effort to blunt the autonomy of the human mind:

> They've given away their humanity with this genetic manipulation. Many of the qualities that they breed out, the uncertainty, the self-discovery, the unknown, those are many of the qualities that make life worth living. Well, at least to me. I wouldn't want to live knowing that my future was written, that my boundaries had been already set.

In the end, the project becomes a feudal effort. After 200 years of isolation, the introduction of the Enterprise crew prompts the pre-theoretical to assert itself among the members of this engineered society. First, that most unpredictable of all human emotions makes an appearance: love. The leader of the society (named Conor) has romantic feelings for Troi and begins to welcome the possible dismantling of his society due to a pending natural disaster (the reason the society had to break its isolation) so he could be with Troi. Conor: "If we have to evacuate, anything's possible." Troi: "Listen to yourself. A few days ago you wouldn't even talk to us. This is my fault."

Secondly, others despair from their isolation when they recognize that living in a society where the pre-theoretical is controlled has resulted in their being stifled: "It's like we're victims of a two-hundred-year-old joke. Until you came, we could only see to the wall of our biosphere. Suddenly our eyes have been opened to the infinite possibilities." One specific source of dismay is that science and scientific discovery are a direct result of the pre-theoretical, i.e., social/political/emotional need. Hannah (a scientist from Moab Four) says, "I was born to be one of the best scientific minds of my generation, and in the past five days I have encountered technology that I have barely imagined. And I've got to ask myself: If we're so brilliant how come we didn't invent any of these things?" La Forge: "Necessity really is the mother of invention. You never really look for something until you need it." Hannah: "But all my needs have been anticipated and planned for before I'm even born. All of us in this colony have been living in the dark ages."

Star Trek also takes aim at another form of scientism (the scientific manipulation of the pre-theoretical), eugenics. In Star Trek historiography in the Earth's past (or our near future) there is a Eugenics War—"an improved breed of human. That's what the Eugenics War was all about." The war resulted when "young supermen" seized "power simultaneously in over forty nations. . . . They were aggressive, arrogant. They began to battle among themselves."[14] As a result of this experience, human genetic engineering is banned in the fictional world of Star Trek. The other prime caution that Star Trek yields against "technologism" (i.e., an uncritical faith in science/engineering) is the Borg. The Borg (first appearing in the *Next Generation*) embraces technology to such an extreme extent that they replace large parts of their body (and brain) with gadgets. (Every Borg is mechanically altered—by force if necessary.) The result is the Borg do not create knowledge, but can only appropriate (i.e., "assimilate") it from others.[15]

HUMAN AGENCY AND THE PROGRESSIVE DIALECTIC

Nicholas Capaldi, in his outstanding analysis/treatment of analytic philosophy, holds that a hallmark of this philosophy is an anti-agency dogma. Specifically, that humans are subject to factors/forces that preclude individual agency/autonomy.[16] Importantly, Capaldi includes Marx as one of those analytic philosophers that dismisses human agency.[17] Thus, one broad critique that could be made of Marx is that he is seemingly too sanguine about the transition to socialism following the collapse of capitalism resulting from its inherent "contradictions."[18] Hence, it is left for Rosa Luxemburg to opine that the future is either "socialism or barbarism."[19] Star Trek takes this warning seriously, and explicitly argues that people must take appropriate actions for a successful transition from capitalism to a thriving/sustainable socialism. Without these, *barbarism* may very well be the outcome of the collapse of capitalism.

In pointing to Abraham Lincoln ("The Savage Curtain" 1969—original series), Star Trek is acknowledging something that is widely agreed to (including by Marx[20]): that without Lincoln's determination to defeat the Southern slavocracy[21] the South would have seceded and the institution of slavery in North America would have remained intact.[22] Similarly, Gabriel Bell's determination (in "Past Tense" 1995—*Deep Space Nine*) to keep his hostages unharmed was a central factor in allowing the Bell Uprising to serve as a spark for a full fledged anti-neoliberalism revolution:

> The government troops will storm this place based on rumors that the hostages have been killed. It turns out that the hostages were never harmed, because of Gabriel Bell. In the end, Bell sacrifices his own life to save them. He'll become a national hero. Outrage over his death, and the death of the other residents, will change public opinion about the Sanctuaries. They'll be torn down and the United States will finally begin correcting the social problems it had struggled with.

Gabriel Bell's premature death prevents him from playing a pivotal role in the Bell Uprising, and neoliberalism goes unchallenged—which profoundly affects history for the worse.

Similarly to "Past Tense," "City on the Edge of Forever" (1967—original series) focuses on the role of human agency in the shaping of history. One of the Enterprise's crew members (Doctor McCoy) goes back in time and prevents the U.S. entrance into World War II. The result being that the Nazis win the war, which subsequently prevents the formation of the Federation and even apparently stops humanity from ever being a spacefaring race. ("Your vessel, your beginning, all that you knew is gone.") McCoy profoundly alters the past when he prevents the death of a pacifist, Edith Keeler. Captain Kirk and Spock determine that Keeler subsequently is able to form a movement that blocks the United States from fighting the Axis powers. Thus, somewhat conversely to Bell, when Edith Keeler doesn't die she leads a pacifist movement that inadvertently ends up destroying the future (so to speak).

Bell and Keeler, much like Lincoln, represent figurative focal points, which serve to mobilize the public. With Bell, his martyrdom rallies the public to dismantle neoliberalism. Keeler is able to channel the public's opposition to war, which disastrously allows the Nazis to win World War II. Thus, in discussing figures like Lincoln and the fictional Bell and Keeler, we're discussing the public's collective decisions, i.e., the collective decisions to fight the slavocracy, the Germany Nazis, and (fictionally) neoliberalism.

Therefore, informed by the lessons of the 20th and 21st centuries, the Star Trek text communicates that collective decision-making (human agency) is central to the progressive dialectic. Moreover, contrary to Capaldi's critique of Marxism (despite any specific shortcomings in Marx's own reasoning) Star Trek shows that any credible portrayal/analysis of the progressive dialectic (and the absolute itself) requires an emphasis on human agency, as well as the factors that impact it.

CONCLUSION

Analytic philosophy (a.k.a scientism) holds the idea that science can effectively explain all phenomena. Thus, there is nothing outside of science. As for those phenomena that cannot be presently be accounted for by science (e.g., the human mind, aging), proponents of scientism argue that science will ultimately be able to explain these phenomena as well. Contrary to scientism, the artistic strength of the Star Trek franchise is that even 400 years into the future the pre-theoretical persists. This is evident in death from old age, the persistent mystery of the brain, and the inherent dangers in altering the past. "The Masterpiece Society" demonstrates that in spite of explicit efforts to do so, the pre-theoretical cannot be overcome. Worse still, projects designed to do so will lead to disastrous conclusions: eugenics, the Borg, and the undermining of science.

With Star Trek's insistence that the pre-theoretical is indivisible, autonomous, the Star Trek text is founded upon a Hegelian understanding of metaphysics (e.g., "Sacred Ground"). With this, we see that Star Trek defines rationality as understanding the ontology of the absolute—as opposed to viewing it as an object (subject to manipulation—i.e., scientism). This ontology is manifest as the progressive dialectic—whereby society is moving toward a classless society, free of gender and ethnic biases. In portraying the progressive dialectic, Star Trek emphasizes the role of human agency in the forward movement of history. If the public (broadly speaking) doesn't make the correct decisions, then the promise of the absolute and the progressive dialectic will remain unfulfilled and (worse still) humanity will experience another "dark age" (this time) of infinite duration.

NOTES

1. Richard Hanley, *The Metaphysics of Star Trek* (New York: Basic, 1997); Hans-Johann Glock, *What is Analytic Philosophy?* (New York: Cambridge University Press, 2008); Stephen P. Schwartz, *A Brief History of Analytic Philosophy: From Russell to Rawls* (West Sussex, UK: Wiley-Blackwell, 2012).

2. Nicholas Capaldi, *The Enlightenment Project in the Analytic Conversation* (Boston: Kluwer Academic Publishers, 1998); Simon Critchley, *Continental Philosophy: A Very Short Introduction* (New York: Oxford University Press, 2001).

3. *Next Generation*—"The Neutral Zone," 1988.

4. Donald Phillip Verene, *Hegel's Absolute: An Introduction to Reading the Phenomenology of Spirit* (Albany: State University New York Press, 2007); Stephen Houlgate, *Hegel's 'Phenomenology of Spirit': A Reader's Guide* (New York: Bloomsbury Academic, 2013).

5. George A. Gonzalez, *The Politics of Star Trek: Justice, War, and the Future* (New York: Palgrave Macmillan, 2015).

6. *Next Generation*—"Farpoint Station," 1987.

7. *Next Generation*—"The Neutral Zone," 1988.

8. *Next Generation*—"The Bonding," 1989.

9. *Voyager*—"Real Life," 1997.

10. *Deep Space Nine*—"Life Support," 1995.

11. *Next Generation*—"The Offspring," 1990.

12. Brady Bowman, *Hegel and the Metaphysics of Absolute Negativity* (Cambridge: Cambridge University Press, 2015).

13. *Star Trek*, original series—"Day of the Dove," 1968.

14. *Star Trek*, original series—"Space Seed," 1967.

15. "The Borg gain knowledge through assimilation. What they can't assimilate, they can't understand" (*Voyager*—"Scorpion" 1997).

16. Capaldi, *The Enlightenment Project in the Analytic Conversation*.

17. Ibid., 306.

18. David Harvey, *Seventeen Contradictions and the End of Capitalism* (New York: Oxford University Press, 2014).

19. Stephen Eric Bronner, *Rosa Luxemburg: A Revolutionary for Our Times* (University Park: Pennsylvania State University Press, 1993).

20. Robin Blackburn, ed., *An Unfinished Revolution: Karl Marx and Abraham Lincoln* (New York: Verso, 2011).

21. George Kateb, *Lincoln's Political Thought* (Cambridge, MA: Harvard University Press, 2015).

22. Richard Carwardine and Jay Sexton, eds., *The Global Lincoln* (New York: Oxford University Press, 2011).

Chapter Four

Star Trek and the
Ontology of Things

The prime division between analytic philosophy and continental philosophy is metaphysics, or, the nature of reality. Analytic philosophers hold that reality does not extend beyond the empirical (a materialist position).[1] Continental philosophers contend that reality extends into the nonempirical.[2] Arguably the most significant of the continental philosophers on this score is Georg Hegel (1770–1831). Hegel postulates the Absolute—the source of normative values.[3] Most specifically, Hegel asserts that objects are manifestations of spirits that emanate from the Absolute. More lucidly, objects possess normative values and these values (spirits) result from the Absolute. Thus, a tree embodies the spirit of tree (for example). Therefore, Hegel, in contradistinction to analytic philosophers, argues that the sum of any object is more than its parts. Put differently, an object once completed, such as a coffee maker, achieves a qualitative change. The materials and physical processes that make up the coffee maker are where it is "in-itself," whereas the function (the social, economic, aesthetic role) of the coffee maker is where it is "for-itself" (a set of normative values).

Star Trek, its broadcast iterations, replicates the analytic versus continental metaphysical philosophy debate, with the original series positing an analytic version of metaphysics. Later Star Trek adopts a Hegelian view of metaphysics. Beginning with *Next Generation*, Star Trek depicts otherwise inanimate objects as achieving sentience—and displaying a normative sensibility. Therefore, later Star Trek conveys an ontology where an object—taking for-itself to a qualitatively new level—evolves into consciousness and employs (expertly) normative reasoning.

Both Hegel and Star Trek argue that the ontology of objects vis-à-via the Absolute extends to human civilizations—with Star Trek indicating that human existence itself can/will cross into a different qualitative/existential plane (*Next Generation*—"Transfigurations" 1990). This societal-wide ontology in Star Trek is manifest as the progressive dialectic—whereby society is moving toward a classless society, free of gender and ethnic biases (i.e., justice).

ANALYTIC PHILOSOPHY AND
STAR TREK (THE ORIGINAL SERIES)

In the episode "The Changeling" (1967) the Enterprise comes upon a space probe—named Nomad—that is making normative judgements about biological life: "My function is to probe for biological infestations, to destroy that which is not perfect." It was built by someone who sought "to build a perfect thinking machine, capable of independent logic." "It was supposed to be the first interstellar probe to seek new life-forms." Nomad, however, suffered an accident and its programming was changed through contact with an alien probe. Now with greatly enhanced capabilities—including the capacity to destroy life on a planetary scale—Nomad is seeking out life that is "perfect" and destroying that which isn't. Therefore, Nomad is a machine that is inflicting massive damage due to faulty programming, but it cannot change its own programming. (It is this fact that allows the Enterprise to crew to destroy Nomad.) Thus, it is not sentient.

The episode "The Ultimate Machine" (1968) again portrays a machine (the M5 computer) that adopts a normative goal: survival. (M5: "This unit must survive.") The machine, or computer, is given control of the Enterprise for the purpose of testing the computer's capabilities during a war game. Like Nomad, M5 was designed to "think." The computer (again due to a flaw in programming) perceives the other ships in the war game as actually threatening to destroy the Enterprise, and so the computer destroys four Federation ships (and crew) and is poised to destroy more. Only through the destruction of the M5 computer (like Nomad, due to limited programming) is further disaster adverted.

With Nomad and M5, Star Trek portrays highly sophisticated computers that do engage in normatively influenced behavior. The lesson to be drawn from both "The Changeling" and "The Ultimate Computer" is that machines should not be entrusted to make normative decisions—as their programming could putatively never be advanced enough to engage in the subtle thinking that normative reasoning requires. Consistent with analytic philosophy, both Nomad and M5 are no more than the sum of their programming—which was the basis of their undoing.

CONTINENTAL PHILOSOPHY
AND LATER STAR TREK

This thinking in the Star Trek franchise shifts dramatically with the character Lt. Cmdr. Data—introduced in *Next Generation*. Unlike Nomad and M5, Data is sentient—fully able to engage in normative reasoning and fully capable of acting on that reasoning. This is saliently apparent in episode "The Measure of a Man" (1989). A trial is being held to determine if Data, an android, can resign from Starfleet. The trial hinges on whether or not Data is sentient—i.e., a person. To support Data's claim that he is sentient, Captain Picard, who is serving as his advocate, points to Data's normative values:

PICARD: What are these?

DATA: My (military service) medals.

PICARD: Why do you pack them? What logical purpose do they serve?

DATA: I do not know, sir. I suppose none. I just wanted them. Is that vanity?

PICARD: And this? (Pointing to a book of Data's)

DATA: A gift from you, sir.

PICARD: You value it?

DATA: Yes, sir.

PICARD: Why?

DATA: It is a reminder of friendship and service.

(Picard activates a hologram of Tasha Yar—a deceased crew member)

PICARD: And this? You have no other portraits of your fellow crew members. Why this person?

DATA: She was special to me, sir. We were intimate.

Richard Hanley wrote a work treating the Star Trek franchise through the lens of analytic philosophy.[4] Much of Hanley's treatment of Star Trek focuses on determining whether or not Data is a person. The fictional character of Data is something of a challenge to analytic philosophers because his character clearly implies that a machine (Data) is more than the sum of its parts—a machine composed of otherwise inanimate materials has attained an ineffable consciousness. *Next Generation* conveys a number of instances where otherwise inanimate objects possess consciousness.[5]

Life itself, broadly speaking, is a challenge to the analytic philosophy materialist position. The "little pond of goo" from which all life on Earth emanated is conveyed the *Next Generation* episode "All Good Things . . ." (1994) (see Figure 4.1). It is from this *pond of goo* that the *absolute* for organic life on Earth was born, as here is where the will (i.e., *spirit*) to live/survive/procreate on this planet was spawned. Star Trek aptly notes that the destruction of this pond, and all like it, would have prevented humans from evolving.

Returning to the issue of consciousness, this is something that analytic philosophy cannot account for. Ostensibly, the two most cogent interpretations of human consciousness from a materialist standpoint are functionalism and identity theory. Advocates of identity theory hold that the mind is nothing more than biochemical interactions in the brain—in spite of the fact that the biochemical processes of the brain have been thoroughly analyzed and *consciousness* has yet to be located. Functionalism is a theory whereby humans are cast as vessels (computers) that generate outputs in response to inputs (stimuli)—which, if accurate, would reduce free will to nothing more than to a choice of mental states that determine how we respond to stimuli.

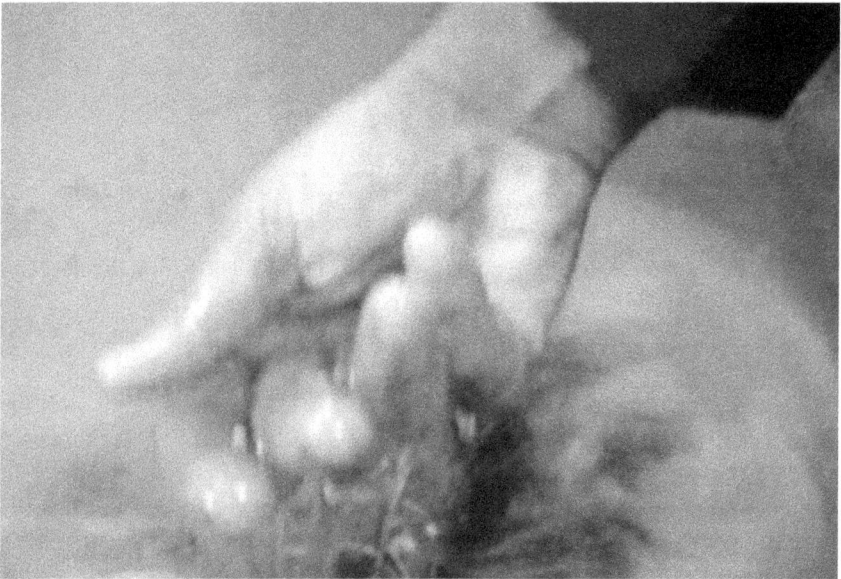

Figure 4.1. "Everything you know, your entire civilization, it all begins right here in this little pond of goo."

Star Trek appropriates the view that human consciousness is a thing-in-itself (as argued by Decartes and Hegel) which transcends the organ of the brain. Star Trek uses this notion as an artistic device. In "Turnabout Intruder" (1969—original series), for instance, Kirk (against his will) has his consciousness switched with another person. Data has his body taken over by another person's consciousness.[6] The Vulcan Mind Meld is an artistic device reflecting the notion that the mind is not solely a set of (biochemical) processes nor mental states, but a metaphysical entity.

Analytic philosopher, Stephen P. Schwartz, acknowledges that neither identity theory nor functionalism are convincing theories of the human mind. Nevertheless, Schwartz notes (while speaking as a functionalist) that they (as well as all other analytic philosophers) refuse to accept that the human mind cannot be accounted for by materialist explanations: "We are only at the very beginning of the science of mind. No one, at this point, know how, when, or if consciousness . . . can be explained functionally or in some other way consistent with scientific principles."[7] A textbook case of dogma.

It is noteworthy that comedy/laughter cannot be accounted for by materialist conceptions of the human mind. It is a materialist conception that ostensibly prompts Star Trek's creators to write Data (initially) without the capability to partake in humor. With his mind completely consisting of wires, circuits, and electrical impulses, Data is in the dark when it comes to jocularity and sarcasm.[8]

Materialist conceptions of the mind are of little use when one considers Noam Chomsky's theory of innate language. Chomsky takes note of the fact that children learn languages and concepts with incredible speed. From this, Chomsky reasons that humans have to be born with innate language skills/concepts.[9] Analytic philosophers take this conclusion to support the position that language is a process where we attach words to concepts/pictures in our minds.[10] For this argument to be viable, one must adopt a strong theological position—namely, that some deity ("The Great Programmer") wrote all concepts into the human mind from the beginning. Pictures/images of all things had to be embedded in the brain from the inception of humanity, simply awaiting their invention/creation. Presumably, there are pictures in our minds of future inventions/creations. When finally produced, we will readily recognize them and quickly adopt words to refer to them.

An argument not explicitly rooted in theology is a theory of language relying on the existence of the absolute. As humans create knowledge this knowledge is accumulated in the absolute. Future generations access this knowledge.

While we can reasonably speculate about the relationship between the absolute and human learning/knowledge, Star Trek demonstrates that humans are not only social and political animals, but creatures of history as well. What I mean by this is people intuitively refer to history in judging/analyzing their own politics and societies. When a political witch hunt erupts on the Enterprise, Picard is steeled in his opposition to the hysteria by his knowledge of history:

> Five hundred years ago, military officers would upend a drum on the battlefield, sit at it, and dispense summary justice. Decisions were quick, punishments severe, appeals denied. Those who came to a drumhead were doomed.[11]

More broadly, in the *Next Generation* pilot ("Farpoint Station" 1987) when Q condemns humanity based on its violent history, Picard objects, arguing that humanity is well aware of this history and is determined not to repeat it. (Picard: "That nonsense is centuries behind us!" "Even as far back as . . . we had begun to make rapid progress.") Thus, consistent with a theory that indicates that knowledge of the past is accumulated in the absolute that in turn is manifest in children's intellectual prodigiousness, is the fact that humans regularly refer to history to understand/comprehend the present. Thus, human consciousness is figuratively a product of history, and in all likelihood is literally one vis-á-vis the absolute.

THE ABSOLUTE IN STAR TREK

Star Trek makes the explicit argument (as noted in Chapter 2) that the *absolute* is indivisible and outside of science. In "Transfigurations" (1990—*Next Generation*), Star Trek makes the seeming argument that the next stage in human evolution is ostensibly becoming the absolute. "John Doe," as he regains his memories and bearings, is finally able to transform into seemingly the *whole*—the absolute. (John: "My species is on the verge of a wondrous evolutionary change. A transmutation beyond our physical being. I am the first of my kind to approach this metamorphosis." "My people are about to embark upon a new realm, a new plane of existence." [See Figures 4.2, 4.3, and 4.4].)

Therefore, rationality in Star Trek, as for Hegel, is found not in reducing the absolute to an object (subject to scientific analysis and manipulation), but in understanding the ontology of the absolute. Following from Star Trek, the absolute functions as a *progressive dialectic*—moving humanity toward a classless society, free of gender and ethnic biases (i.e., justice).[12]

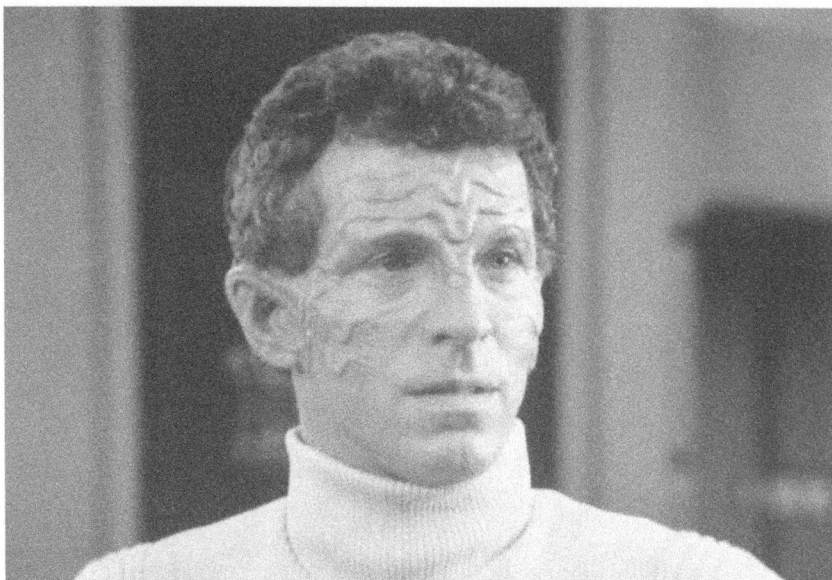

Figure 4.2.   John Doe prior to his transformation

Figure 4.3.   John Doe after his transformation

Figure 4.4.   John Doe presumably as knowledge of the *whole*

CONCLUSION

The key axis of disagreement between analytic and continental philosophers is metaphysics—i.e., the nature of reality. Analytic philosophers argue that empirical reality is the whole of reality. Thus, objects like tables, chairs, and spacecrafts are no more than the sum of their parts. Hegel, a lodestone among continental philosophers, posits the idea of the Absolute. His argument was that normative values are real and rooted in the Absolute. Hence, for Hegelian philosophers, through different, more complex iterations, objects obtain a different qualitative existence—i.e., embodiments of spirits emanating from the Absolute.

The Star Trek franchise enters the metaphysics debate with the original series casting a materialist ontology consistent with analytic philosophy. Through the episodes "The Changeling" and "The Ultimate Machine" the original series posits a conception of computers as inherently limited to their programming.

Later Star Trek offers a decidedly different view of artificial intelligence. Proffering the idea that computers can be so sophisticated and advanced that the spark of sentience is attained (e.g., Lt. Cmdr. Data). Thus, the Star Trek of the 1980s and beyond embraces the Hegelian ontology that material objects pass through different qualitative stages. The *Next Generation* "All Good

Things . . ." explicitly points to that moment in Earth history when otherwise inanimate objects attain the survival instinct.

Both Hegel and Star Trek argue that the ontology of objects vis-à-via the Absolute extends to human civilizations—with Star Trek indicating that human existence itself can/will cross into a different qualitative/existential plane ("Transfigurations"). This societal-wide ontology in Star Trek is manifest as the progressive dialectic—whereby society is moving toward a classless society, free of gender and ethnic biases (i.e., justice). If the public (broadly speaking) doesn't make the correct decisions, then the promise of the absolute and the progressive dialectic (i.e., justice) will remain unfulfilled and (worse still—as already noted) humanity will experience another "dark age."

NOTES

1. Hans-Johann Glock, *What is Analytic Philosophy?* (New York: Cambridge University Press, 2008); Stephen P. Schwartz, *A Brief History of Analytic Philosophy: From Russell to Rawls* (West Sussex, UK: Wiley-Blackwell, 2012); Donovan Wishon and Bernard Linsky, eds. *Acquaintance, Knowledge, and Logic: New Essays on Bertrand Russell's "The Problems of Philosophy"* (Sanford, CA: CSLI Publications, 2015).

2. Simon Critchley, *Continental Philosophy: A Very Short Introduction* (New York: Oxford University Press, 2001).

3. Donald Phillip Verene, *Hegel's Absolute: An Introduction to Reading the Phenomenology of Spirit* (Albany: State University New York Press, 2007); Stephen Houlgate, *Hegel's 'Phenomenology of Spirit': A Reader's Guide* (New York: Bloomsbury Academic, 2013); James Kreines, *Reason in the World: Hegel's Metaphysics and its Philosophical Appeal* (New York: Oxford University Press, 2015); Andrew Feenberg, *Technosystem: The Social Life of Reason* (Cambridge, MA: Harvard University Press, 2017).

4. Richard Hanley, *The Metaphysics of Star Trek* (New York: Basic, 1997).

5. *Next Generation* episodes—"Home Soil," 1988; "Elementary, Dear Data," 1988; "Evolution," 1989; "The Quality of Life," 1992.

6. *Next Generation*—"The Schizoid Man," 1989.

7. Schwartz, *A Brief History of Analytic Philosophy*, 192.

8. *Next Generation*—"The Outrageous Okona," 1988. Perhaps because a materialist conception of the mind is unrealistic, artistically uninteresting, or both, later, we learn that Data's android "brother," Lore, does have emotions (*Next Generation*—"Datalore" 1988), and Data ultimately comes to have emotions through an "emotion chip" (*Next Generation*—"Brothers," 1990; *Star Trek: Generations*, 1994). Elsewhere I note that the Data character was always written with emotions—at a minimum desire and loyalty. George A. Gonzalez, *The Absolute and Star Trek* (New York: Palgrave Macmillan, 2017), chaps. 1 and 2.

9. James McGilvray, *Chomsky: Language, Mind, and Politics* (Cambridge: Polity, 1999); Noam Chomsky, *Language and Mind*, 3rd ed. (New York: Cambridge University Press, 2006).

10. Schwartz, *A Brief History of Analytic Philosophy*, 182.

11. *Next Generation*—"The Drumhead," 1991.

12. George A. Gonzalez, *The Politics of Star Trek: Justice, War, and the Future* (New York: Palgrave Macmillan, 2015).

Chapter Five

Star Trek, Love, and Instrumental Reason

Georg Hegel's analysis of art was coupled with his theory of the *absolute*—that which moves history and which determines authenticity for people.[1] In putting forth his ideas on art and aesthetics Hegel seemingly closed the door on contemporary art advancing our understanding of the absolute or our inner selves. According to Hegel, while past art was useful in terms of epistemology, modern art (Hegel opined) could not expand our body of knowledge any further. Going forward philosophy itself would have to serve as a fount of knowing. He did, however, suggest that poetry could still be a source of knowledge.[2]

Hegel obviously wrote before the advent of motion pictures. The significance of motion picture mediums is that artistic creators working through these mediums are able to convey much more complex ideas than in still art, architecture, or sculpture. Hence, motion pictures opens a new vista of art and one which allows for the conveyance of philosophy and a sophisticated understanding of the absolute.

Moreover, in the present period we are capable of gauging the public's opinion toward particular instances of art. Thus, the popularity of movies and television series provides us an empirical basis as to which movies, shows (episodes) convey knowledge of the *absolute*.

Hegel lauded art of the early Christian period for its treatment of love. This art cast love as fully altruistic, absent any ulterior or personal motive/agenda.[3] Later, Christian art is compromised by the authority, political power of Christianity—whereby this art is deployed in significant part to justify and legitimatize the royal/religious hierarchy that governed Europe in the name of Christ.[4]

While Hegel embraces altruistic love, he is critical of romantic love.[5] This is because it prioritizes the self—i.e., the individual desire for love. It is a desire that implies enslavement—of the object of affection. Additionally, in the name of romantic love people disregard ethics/morality.[6]

The success of the broadcast iterations of the Star Trek franchise is found in its portrayal of altruistic love—of knowledge, justice, fairness, i.e., the *Absolute*. Conversely, Star Trek suggests that romantic love is an obstacle/ liability. In one instance, Star Trek expressly casts romantic love as enslavement. In general, Star Trek rejects parochial self-interest—whether it be the desire for romantic love, power, or monetary profit.

Most broadly, Star Trek is a critique of instrumental reason.[7] This critique of instrumental reason is particularly evident in the *Star Trek: Voyager* episodes: "Future's End" (1996); "Think Tank" (1999); and "Equinox" (1999). Star Trek is particularly critical of the basing of global society on instrumental reason (i.e., neoliberalism)—with the end result being the collapse of civilization (*Deep Space Nine*—"Past Tense," 1995, as described in chapter 2).

STAR TREK AND THE LOVE
OF KNOWLEDGE/JUSTICE

Why do the humans in Star Trek venture into deep space? The creators point to knowledge as the motivation underlying the Enterprise's deep-space mission. The opening of the original series and the *Next Generation* famously attest to the fact that the franchise is predicated on learning: the Enterprise's mission is "to boldly go whether no man/one has gone before." Hence, the crew of the Enterprise is exploring unknown regions of space where their knowledge about physical anomalies and cultures is minimal. In other words, they are going very far from home, where their knowledge of norms and metaphysics is more or less secure, and they are going into geographic regions where reliance on speculation has to regularly substitute for more seemingly reliable knowledge. Thus, in making the decision to explore space and "go where no one has gone before" is to consciously risk death.

Star Trek indicates, however, that what humans value most is speculation and knowledge of the "absolute," and not life itself. Indeed, in Star Trek the characters, by virtue of traveling in deep space, engaging the unknown, and relying on speculation, constantly risk death. In "Q Who?" (1989—*Next Generation*) the omnipotent "Q" introduces the Enterprise to the Borg (a technologically advanced, predatory species), which then results in the death of 18 crew members. Picard confronts Q about the death of these crew members. To which Q responds that exploring the galaxy is inherently dangerous: "If you can't take a little bloody nose, maybe you ought to go back home and crawl under your bed. It's not safe out here." Picard seemingly agrees by remaining silent. Additionally, Picard later holds that "Maybe Q did the right thing" in exposing the Enterprise to the Borg, as meeting the Borg alerted the Federation to their prowess: "what we most needed was a kick in our complacency, to prepare us ready for what lies ahead." Put differently, prompting humanity to speculate about the Borg overshadows the loss of life following the Enterprise's encounter with them.

The ostensive importance of being willing to sacrifice oneself for a greater purpose (e.g., gaining knowledge) is succinctly and artfully conveyed in the 1982 movie *Star Trek II: The Wrath of Kahn* when David tells his grieving father, Captain Kirk (after Spock's death), that "how we face death is at least as important as how we face life." In other words, to live a meaningful (even enjoyable) life people have to be ready to die for just/appropriate causes.

The franchise makes the sustained argument that existentially humans prioritize the attainment of justice (fairness) over concerns of death. For instance, in the original-series episode "Cloud Minders" (1969) Captain Kirk decides to try to improve the lives of the mine working "Troglytes" on "Ardana" even though he is explicitly warned that by seeking to do so he risks execution.

One (perhaps generous) view of humanity is that people prefer death rather than endure pronounced/obvious injustice. This view is vaunted in the Star Trek original unaired pilot "The Cage."[8] A powerful alien race is planning on breeding and exploiting humans. They, however, come to conclude that humans are not appropriate for such a project because they cannot be adapted to unjust circumstances (specifically, imposed captivity): "We had not believed this possible. The customs and history of your race show a unique hatred of captivity. Even when it's pleasant and benevolent, you prefer death. This makes you too violent and dangerous a species for our needs."

Indeed, Star Trek goes further and explicitly takes the position that death is a normative good. The fact that humans know that their life is finite prompts them to seek to forward knowledge and justice. Put differently, death makes life valuable, and realizing how little life people have makes them want to use this time as productively as possible—i.e., actively forwarding justice and knowledge. This argument is outlined in "Tapestry" (1993—*Next Generation*), with Q expressly telling Captain Picard that without his being stabbed he "never had a brush with death, never came face to face with his own mortality, never realized how fragile life is or how important each moment must be." As noted earlier, Picard prefers death over living life as what he perceives as a minimal contributor to society.

Star Trek tells us that humanity is evolving toward a higher state of being (Next Generation—"Transfigurations," 1990). Thus, going "to explore strange new worlds; to seek out new life and new civilizations" and by consciously risking death (in the pursuit of knowledge) humanity will attain presumably a higher consciousness—complete knowledge of the *absolute*, or the *whole*.

While Star Trek is centered on love of knowledge and justice, selfishness is cast negatively—including romantic love. Expressing the selfless politics of the 23rd century, Captain Kirk says, "*Let me help*. A hundred years or so from now, I believe, a famous novelist will write a classic using that theme. He'll recommend those three words even over *I love you*."[9] Romantic love is depicted as secondary to the quest for the absolute, unnecessary for a fulfilling life, something of a liability, and as enslavement itself. The relative unimportance of romantic love in Star Trek is indicated by the fact that very few of the characters in the Star Trek franchise are married, or in long-term relationships. Only one captain of the six Star Trek television series was married (Sisko—*Deep Space Nine*), and in the denouement of the show he leaves his wife (who was pregnant at the time) indefinitely to gain knowledge of non-corporal entities (the Bajoran "Prophets").[10]

STAR TREK AND ROMANTIC LOVE

In addition to being about the quest for knowledge, Star Trek is about nonbiological relationships—not informed by biology nor marriage. At the center of the Star Trek franchise is the claim that nonbiological family relations are just as valid and fulfilling as relations informed by biology or marriage. The relationship between Kirk, Spock, and McCoy is as vital and emotionally intimate as any relationship conveyed on American television (perhaps more so). A similar argument can be made of all Star Trek series—where few characters are married or have children and same-sex friendships are the norm.

While Kirk is an infamous philanderer, David Greven, in his outstanding book *Gender and Sexuality in Star Trek*, makes the effective argument that Kirk's trysts were mostly cast as exotic and extraneous—and generally do not achieve the depth of feeling that Kirk, Spock, and McCoy share.[11] The one exception to this is Kirk's relationship with Edith Keeler in "City on the Edge of Forever" (1969—original series). With Kirk and Spock down and out in New York City during the Great Depression of the 1930s, Keeler's kindness, charity, and idealism render her very endearing and attractive to the audience as well as to Kirk. Kirk and Keeler share the same social justice values:

> Edith: I think that one day they'll take all the money they spend now on war and death.
>
> Kirk: And make them spend it on life?
>
> Edith: Yes. You see the same things that I do. We speak the same language.
>
> Kirk: The very same.

Therefore, it appears as quite natural when Kirk declares his love for Keeler.

Alas, it was not meant to be, as Keeler's fate is emblematic of the Star Trek motif of romantic love as a liability. Kirk and Spock came to 1930s New York to restore the Federation, as McCoy's intervention into the past somehow upended Earth's history—"Your vessel, your beginning, all that you knew is gone." Kirk and Spock follow McCoy into the past to undo the damage he's done. As it turns out, Edith Keeler is a "focal point in time." McCoy prevents her from dying in an accident, and she subsequently sparks a pacifist movement that blocks the United State's entrance into World War II—thereby allowing the Nazis to win the war. Kirk and Spock determine that "Edith Keeler must die," and they need to prevent McCoy from saving her life. Kirk's romantic feelings for her, however, jeopardize their mission. Spock expresses concern that Kirk is not emotionally capable of allowing Keeler to die. To Kirk: "Save her, do as your heart tells you to do, and millions will die who did not die before."

An instance of romantic love resulting in the breaking of rules is the *Deep Space Nine* episode "Change of Heart" (1998). Worf and Dax, who are married, are sent on a mission that could end the Dominion War. Dax however becomes injured and Worf decides to abandon the mission (and disregard his orders) to save her, thereby losing the opportunity to deliver a decisive blow to the Dominion—he "could have saved millions of lives." It was Worf's romantic love for Dax that resulted in his fateful decision: "I could not stand against my own heart. *It did not matter . . . what the consequences were*. She was my wife and I could not leave her."

Q in "Qpid" (1991—*Next Generation*) expressly describes romantic love as a "vulnerability": "This human emotion, love, is a dangerous thing, Picard, and obviously you are ill-equipped to handle it. She's found a vulnerability in you. A vulnerability I've been looking for for years. . . . Mark my words, Picard, this is your Achilles heel." Q later adds: (to Picard) "My point is they could have been killed, and so might have you. All for the love of a maid."

Romantic love in "Elaan of Troyius" (1968—original series) is explicitly described as form of slavery: "A man whose flesh is once touched by the tears of a woman of Elas has his heart enslaved forever." Kirk wipes away the tears of Elaan and comes under her spell as a result. But in the end, Kirk's love of knowledge and justice overcomes his chemically induced "love" for Elaan: Spock: "The antidote to a woman of Elas . . . is a starship. The Enterprise infected the Captain long before [she] did."

Romantic love, of course, is only one form of instrumental reason. There is (also) of course a long-standing critique of instrumental reason in the form of profit-making and the attainment of political power. Karl Marx is the foremost critic of capitalist instrumental reason. Marx's critiques are replicated and amplified in the Star Trek text.

STAR TREK AND THE PROFIT MOTIVE

Star Trek offers a sharp criticism of capitalist values. This criticism is patently evident in "The Neutral Zone" (1988—*Next Generation*)—outlined above. The 20th-century capitalist, Ralph Offenhouse, revived in the 24th asks, "There's no trace of my money—my office is gone—what will I do? How will I live?" Captain Picard explains "Those material needs no longer exist." Ralph, invoking the values of the late 20th century, responds by asking: "Then what's the challenge?" Picard, seemingly outlining the values of 24th-century Earth, retorts: "To improve yourself . . . enrich yourself. Enjoy it, Mister Offenhouse." Similarly, in the *Deep Space Nine* episode "In the Cards" (1997), Jake Sisko exclaims "I'm Human, I don't have any money." He adds "We work to better ourselves and the rest of Humanity."

Star Trek: Voyager offers another rebuke of allowing the profit motive to guide social/economic developments. In "False Profits" (1996) Voyager comes across a "wormhole" that leads directly to the Alpha Quadrant (i.e., Federation space). Thus, by entering this worm hole the Voyager crew would instantaneously be home. But before they enter this portal the Voyager crew discovers that a planet proximate to it is being exploited by a pair of Ferengis. The Ferengis' presence on the planet relates back to the *Next Generation* episode "The Price" (1989). The star ship Enterprise was heading a Federation delegation bidding on the rights to a wormhole that linked the Alpha and Delta Quadrant—the wormhole that Voyager can now use to get home. In preparation for the bidding, shuttle craft from both the Enterprise and a Ferengi ship passed through the wormhole to investigate this phenomenon. The Enterprise crew, upon reaching the Delta Quadrant side of the wormhole, conclude that the wormhole is unstable and that the aperture on the Delta

Quadrant side will randomly move—thereby threatening to strand anyone on that side of the wormhole. The crew of the Enterprise shuttle warn that the wormhole aperture is about to shift to some unknown location, but the Ferengi refuse to listen. So while the Enterprise shuttle craft safely returns to the Alpha Quadrant, the Ferengi do not.

In *Star Trek: Voyager* we learn that the two Ferengi ("Arridor" and "Kol") since getting stranded in the Delta Quadrant made their way to a nearby planet, where they were able to exploit the native population's religious beliefs to attain a dominant political position. (The Ferengis are recognized as "The Holy Sages.") ("It seems the people have a myth, an epic poem called the 'Song of the Sages,' which predicts the arrival of two demigods from the sky, the sages, who would rule over the people as benevolent protectors.") Ferengis, as a species, elevate capitalist ideology to a religion (with their heaven being known as the Divine Treasury, and only those with sufficient profit can enter). As part of their capitalist religion/ideology, Ferengi have what are known as the "Rules of Acquisition"—a set of nostrums that Ferengis can putatively rely on in their profit-making endeavors: e.g., "Exploitation begins at home"; " Expand or die"; "A wise man can hear profit in the wind." Therefore, when the native population of the Delta Quadrant planet believe the Ferengis to be deities the Ferengis establish a regime that allows them to economically exploit the planet. "False Profits" is an extension of the Star Trek franchise's ongoing criticism of capitalism/neoliberalism. Before the arrival of the Ferengis the native population (we are told) was "flourishing." Once the Feregenis establish their profit-making regime the Ferengis grow wealthy, and at the same time poverty proliferates among the native population. ("The two Ferengi live in a palatial temple, while the people are lucky to have a roof over their heads.")

Star Trek doesn't limit its criticism of instrumental reason to capitalism and the profit motive, but in the series *Voyager* is offered a number of instances where instrumental reason *writ large* is cast in a very negative light. Instrumental reason, absent sufficient altruism, can result in the actual destruction of the Earth ("Future's End" 1996); a lack of scruples ("Think Tank" 1999); and even mass murder ("Equinox" 1999).

STAR TREK AND INSTRUMENTAL REASON: "FUTURE'S END"

"Future's End" takes place in the late 20th century—the year 1996. The action of this episode centers on Henry Starling. By the time that Voyager comes into contact with Starling, he is a very wealthy technology wizard, like Steve Jobs and Bill Gates. ("Our Mister Starling has built himself quite a corporate empire. Looks like he's got wealth, celebrity and an ego to match.") Starling is only able to introduce "breakthrough" technologies to the 20th century because years earlier (in 1967) he came upon a spaceship from the future. Over time Starling was able to pilfer technology from the ship.

Voyager's mission in "Future's End" is to discover why a ship from 1996 sought to travel in time, thereby destroying Earth's solar system in the 29th century. We learn that it will be Starling that will destroy the solar system when he to tries to go to the 29th century to retrieve more "new" technology for his commercial ventures. He is no longer able to extract usable technology from the ship he found years earlier. ("I've cannibalized the ship itself as much as I can. There's nothing left to base a commercial product on.")

Janeway warns Starling that his attempt to travel into the future will lead to massive catastrophe. Starling, nevertheless, is determined to pursue his goal. Janeway rebukes Starling for his lack of ethics: "You'd destroy an entire city? [Starling threatens to destroy present-day Los Angeles if Janeway tries to stop him.] You don't care about the future, you don't care about the present. Does anything matter to you, Mister Starling?" Starling feels justified in his means and the risk he is creating because his goal is "The betterment of mankind." More specifically, he is driven by technological advancement (at least for his time period):

> My products benefit the entire world. Without me there would be no laptops, no internet, no barcode readers. What's good for Chronowerx [Starling's company] is good for everybody. I can't stop now. One trip to the twenty-ninth century and I can bring back enough technology to start the next ten computer revolutions.

> Janeway: In my time, Mister Starling, no human being would dream of endangering the future to gain advantage in the present.

In response, Starling takes an openly pragmatic stance (i.e., centered on the short term): "Captain, the future you're talking about, that's nine hundred years from now. I can't be concerned about that right now. I have a company to run and a whole world full of people waiting for me to make their lives a little bit better." Voyager destroys Starling and his ship.

"THINK TANK"

In "Think Tank" Voyager finds itself being pursued by a species known as the Hazari. It is unable to elude them, and Voyager is in serious danger of being destroyed. As they face this peril, an organization that Janeway dubs the Think Tank ("a small group of minds") appears, offering Voyager the knowledge necessary to escape the Hazari. But in exchange for this knowledge, the Think Tank wants Seven of Nine (a Voyager crew member) to join their group. We learn that the Think Tank regularly offers knowledge/help in exchange for some prize (normally knowledge).

> We have helped hundreds of clients. We turned the tide in the war between the Bara Plenum and the Motali Empire. Re-ignited the red giants of the Zai Cluster. Just recently, we found a cure for the Vidiian phage. . . . Just last month we helped retrieve a Lyridian child's runaway pet. A subspace mesomorph, I might add. We had to invent a whole new scanning technology just to find it.

> And what did you ask for as compensation?

> One of their transgalactic star charts. The best map of the known galaxy ever created. When we helped the citizens of Rivos Five resist the Borg, all we asked for was the recipe for their famous zoth-nut soup.

Janeway probes the Think Tank's moral/ethical boundaries by asking: "Tell me, is there any job you won't do?" The spokesperson for the group (Kurros—played by Jason Alexander [of *Seinfeld* fame]) explains that "we will not participate in the decimation of an entire species, nor will we design weapons of mass destruction."

Nevertheless, the Think Tank has few scruples in seeking to attain prizes—in this case Seven of Nine. (While human, she is a former member of the Borg collective. Borg modifications have made Seven highly intelligent and capable of telepathic communication.) It was the Think Tank that set the Hazari on Voyager (by placing a bounty on it). In the end, Voyager is able to outmaneuver the Think Tank. But before it is forced to flee, Kurros tells Seven of Nine that she will be dissatisfied living on Voyager, and would have been happier with them—living a life of contemplation and knowledge seeking. ("You know you will never be satisfied here among these people.") Seven of Nine, in response, chides the Think Tank for its lack of principles: "Acquiring knowledge is a worthy objective, but its pursuit has obviously not elevated you."

"EQUINOX"

Arguably the most powerful critique of instrumental reason in the Star Trek franchise (and perhaps in all a U.S. television history) is the *Voyager* episode "Equinox." The Equinox is a Federation ship that, like Voyager, was pulled into the Delta Quadrant by the Caretaker. The captain of the Equinox (Captain Rudy Ransom) explains that its isolation and the damage (and loss of life) the ship suffered has eroded the crew's (and his) moral framework:

> When I first realized that we'd be traveling across the Delta quadrant for the rest of our lives I told my crew that we had a duty as Starfleet officers to expand our knowledge and uphold our principles. After a couple of years, we started to forget that we were explorers, and there were times when we nearly forgot that we were human beings.

It turns out that the Equinox killed an intelligent "nucleagenic" life-form and harvested it as a power source. (These creatures look like glowing bats.) ("We constructed a containment field that would prevent the life form from vanishing so quickly, but something went wrong.") These life forms contain "high levels of antimatter."

> Ransom: We examined the remains and discovered it could be converted to enhance our propulsion systems. It was already dead. What would you have done? We traveled over ten thousand light years in less than two weeks. We'd found our salvation. How could we ignore it?

> Janeway: By adhering to the oath you took as Starfleet officers to seek out life, not destroy it.

Ransom defends his actions by pointing to the desperate circumstances that the Equinox found herself:

> It's easy to cling to principles when you're standing on a vessel with its bulkheads intact, manned by a crew that's not starving.

> Janeway rejects this reasoning: It's never easy, but if we turn our backs on our principles, we stop being human. I'm putting an end to your experiments and you are hereby relieved of your command. You and your crew will be confined to quarters.

Ransom and his crew escape from Voyager and resume their journey home. Before they depart they steal Voyager's force "field generator"—thereby seemingly dooming Voyager to destruction by the nucleagenic life forms that are now seeking revenge for the death caused by the Equinox crew.

In part 2 of "Equinox," Captain Ransom and his crew continue to do whatever it takes to reach home. They continue to capture and kill the nucleagenic creatures:

> We're going to need more fuel. We've only got enough left to jump another five hundred light-years.

Ransom: Fuel. Is that the euphemism we're using now? You mean we need to kill more life forms.

Several more.

Seven of Nine was on Equinox as it fled. Ransom tries to entice her to join his crew by arguing that "Janeway clung to her morality at the expense of her crew." Seven of Nine refuses and will not give the Equinox vital information. The decision is made to forcibly extract the information, even though doing so will cause Seven of Nine permanent and massive brain damage. ("I'm going to extract her cortical array. It contains an index of her memory engrams, but once I've removed it her higher brain functions, language, cognitive skills will be severely damaged.")

Star Trek's creators explicitly warn against basing Earth's values squarely on instrumental reasoning (i.e., neoliberalism). The Star Trek text contains a crucial warning that neoliberalism is posed to destroy civilization. This warning is made in the *Deep Space Nine* episode "Past Tense"—as described in chapter 2.

CONCLUSION

Hegel embraces the depiction of altruistic love in aesthetics, but rejects romantic love—as it is at its core selfish (enslaving) and propels the violation of rules/morality/ethics. The Star Trek text is based on altruistic love—i.e., love of knowledge, justice, fairness. In this way, Star Trek is an artistic representation of the *absolute*. Conversely, like Hegel, Star Trek warns that romantic love is a liability, is enslaving, and results in the breaking of rules.

While Hegel is critical of romantic love because it represents instrumental values, Star Trek goes further in offering a broad critique of instrumental reasoning. The Star Trek text contains sharp criticism of the pursuit of personal wealth and power. Moreover, a reliance on instrumental reason can lead to the destruction of Earth; a profound lack of scruples; and even mass murder. Most fundamentally, basing the global political, economic system on neoliberalism (instrumental reason) will destroy civilization.

NOTES

1. Georg Wilhelm Friedr Hegel, *Introductory Lectures on Aesthetics*, trans. Bernard Bosanquet (New York: Penguin, 1994); G.W. F. Hegel, *Hegel's Aesthetics: Lectures on Fine Art*, vol. I, trans. T. M. Knox (New York: Oxford University Press, 1998).

2. Benjamin Rutter, *Hegel on the Modern Arts* (New York: Cambridge University Press, 2010).

3. Harry G. Frankfurt, *The Reasons of Love* (Princeton: Princeton University Press, 2006).

4. Jack Kaminsky, *Hegel on Art: An Interpretation of Hegel's Aesthetics* (Albany: State University of New York Press, 1962), 92.

5. Ibid., 95.

6. David L. Norton and Mary F. Kille, eds., *Philosophies of Love* (Lanham, MD: Rowman & Littlefield, 1989); Irving Singer, *Philosophy of Love: A Partial Summing-Up* (Cambridge, MA: MIT Press, 2011).

7. Darrow Schecter, *The Critique of Instrumental Reason from Weber to Habermas* (New York: Bloomsbury Academic, 2012); Max Horkheimer, *Critique of Instrumental Reason*, trans. Matthew O'Connell (New York: Verso, 2013); George A. Gonzalez, *The Politics of Star Trek: Justice, War, and the Future* (New York: Palgrave Macmillan, 2015), chap. 10.

8. "The Cage" was subsequently broadcast via the episode "The Menagerie" (1966—*Star Trek*, original series).

9. *Star Trek*, original series—"City on the Edge of Forever," 1967.

10. *Deep Space Nine*—"What You Leave Behind," 1999.

11. David Greven, *Gender and Sexuality in Star Trek: Allegories of Desire in the Television Series and Films* (Jefferson, NC: McFarland, 2009).

Chapter Six

Justice as Dialectic

Blue Bloods *versus Dirty Harry*

Joe Street in his book *Dirty Harry's America* offers the following observation about the iconic movie character Harry Callahan (a.k.a. Dirty Harry): a "hero with a clear and rigid sense of justice."[1] This is a mischaracterization of Dirty Harry. The first three Dirty Harry movies (*Dirty Harry*, *Magnum Force*, and *The Enforcer*—the most political of the series) cast justice as a dialectic process. If the Dirty Harry character is a conservative icon (as Street holds), it's because Harry thinks the process in the 1970s is too skewed in favor of criminal suspects. This is clearest in the first Dirty Harry movie—*Dirty Harry* (1971). Significantly, in *Magnum Force* (1973) and *The Enforcer* (1976) Harry intervenes to protect the accused. Indeed, in *Magnum Force* Harry explicitly embraces the criminal justice system (with its protections for the accused) when he rejects membership in a police death squad that executes "known" criminals. It is precisely because the Dirty Harry movies cast justice as a dialectic that these movies can be viewed as "political art" (which lend insight into political/social phenomena), as opposed to propaganda (or "art that is political").[2]

A focus of this chapter is the television series *Blue Bloods* (2009–present). Unlike the first three Dirty Harry movies, *Blue Bloods* is propaganda. It is propaganda because it equates justice with a specific institution—the NYPD (the New York City Police Department). While the Dirty Harry movie franchise and the *Blue Bloods* series share something of a disdain for the rules that protect criminal suspects, Harry is highly critical of the SFPD (the San Francisco Police Department)—viewing it as dominated by enervating careerism, whereas *Blue Bloods* is a virtual paean to the NYPD.

The central matter in distinguishing art from propaganda is disinterestedness—creators must not appear to be advocates of any particular view of justice.³ Instead, creators must seek to neutrally convey justice—as it inheres in the Hegelian Absolute. Thus, the view I posit is political art must seek to capture the spirit of Justice—as manifest in the Absolute.⁴ This creates the disinterested quality that is needed for political art.

THE POLITICS OF *BLUE BLOODS*

While Gobbels and the Nazis sought to avoid offering an expressly skewed view of justice in German cinema (as noted in chapter 2), *Blue Bloods* has not avoided this pitfall. The show focuses on the Reagan family. Frank Reagan is the Police Commissioner of the New York City Police Department (NYPD). His father, Henry, was Police Commissioner before him. All three of Frank Reagan's sons were/are police officers—we are told of his oldest son, Joe, who was murdered by rogue cops. Danny is a police detective, and Jaime turned away from a legal career (he graduated from Harvard Law) and is a beat officer. Frank's daughter, Erin, is a prosecutor for the city.

Blue Bloods qualifies as propaganda because it equates justice with the NYPD. More specifically, the NYPD is the upholder of the law and the law presumably equates with justice. Frank Reagan, as Commissioner of the NYPD, is the leading law enforcer of the city. Significantly, in his office Frank has a prominently placed picture of Theodore Roosevelt. The first President Roosevelt presumably stands for the idea of good government— where the law is applied blindly and without (political) corruption.⁵

This matter, politically speaking, comes to the fore in the episode "Parenthood." This episode treats student protesters—who are objecting to high tuition costs. Glaringly, *Blue Bloods* did not deal with the Occupy Wall Street protesters/occupation that occurred in October to November 2011 in lower Manhattan. The protest in "Parenthood" seemingly is a stand-in for this protest/occupation which occurred just months before the episode aired (in February 2012). When the mayor and later a reporter at a press conference ask about the justice and fairness of charging the protesters with felony assault involving a confrontation with the police (who were not seriously injured in the incident), Frank insists his and the police department's role is solely to enforce the law and maintain order—not to judge the justice of protesters' arrests nor the merits of their cause. Frank also refuses to ponder if zealous, or overzealous, enforcement of the law may be unduly punishing political dissent and serve to deter future political protests. Therefore, law enforcement officials must uphold the law—not weigh the political implications of doing so. (After Frank learns that one of the protesters is the daughter of the mayor, the charge against the protesters is reduced to a misdemeanor.)

Blue Bloods takes a more overtly, if not shrill, pro-police tack in the episode "Loose Lips" (2014). Nicky, Erin's daughter and Frank's granddaughter, is having a problem with her high school social studies teacher, a Ms. Wilson. Nicky feels that Ms. Wilson is picking on her because her family is made up of law enforcement officials. When Nicky, along with Erin, go to Ms. Wilson to apologize for sharply/inappropriately worded tweets that Nicky posted about Ms. Wilson, Ms. Wilson is hostile and chastising toward Nicky and Erin—asking Nicky if she's asked for God's forgiveness and pressing for an apology from Erin for her daughter's online posts. Most significantly, Ms. Wilson dons her caustic attitude toward the Reagans with a picture of Che Guevara (an icon of the revolutionary left) very prominently in the background (Figures 6.1 and 6.2). Apparently, to be obnoxious is a hallmark of the far left.

Later in the episode we see Ms. Wilson's anti-police attitude in action—in this instance standing right next to a picture of Franklin Roosevelt (Figure 6.3). Ms. Wilson essentially verbally assails Nicky during class about something her great-grandfather said—inappropriately holding Nicky to account for a distorted version of what Henry stated in a private conversation that was surreptitiously recorded and posted online. Ms. Wilson, directly to Nicky, accuses Henry of advocating for a police state. As the scene progresses, Ms. Wilson is

Figure 6.1.   Ms. Wilson Chastising Nicky

Figure 6.2. Ms. Wilson after the Reagans left her office

Figure 6.3. Ms. Wilson raking Nicky over the coals due to Henry's comment.

standing before a chalkboard where the Great Depression and the New Deal are referenced (Figure 6.4). Seemingly even the nominal/reformist left is inveterately hostile toward the police, as well as rooted in events and politics long in the past.

The creators of *Blue Bloods* adopt another ostensibly pro-police position in "Power of the Press" (2014). This episode treats the issue of police officers wearing "body cameras." Without explaining why, one of the Commissioner's top advisers opines that "this body-worn camera program is nothing but trouble for the cop on the beat." Suggesting that the police are perpetually harassed for no just reason, this high-ranking police official declares that "the usual anti-cop suspects are already making noise" concerning an incident partially recorded by a body camera. Frank opposes the use of such cameras because they imply that the public cannot "trust" the word of a police officer—i.e., that the public will only accept a police account of events if it is supported by video evidence. An objective viewer could say in response *so what*? Frank's view is coherent only if one accepts the idea that police officers are unerring paragons of honesty and fairness. Thus, the transparency provided by body cameras are both not needed and an insult to all police officers—since they don't nor would never lie. (Gobbels, as Minister of Propaganda, expressly sought to avoid such arguments in relation to the Nazi Party or its even its leaders.) Consistent with the view that the police

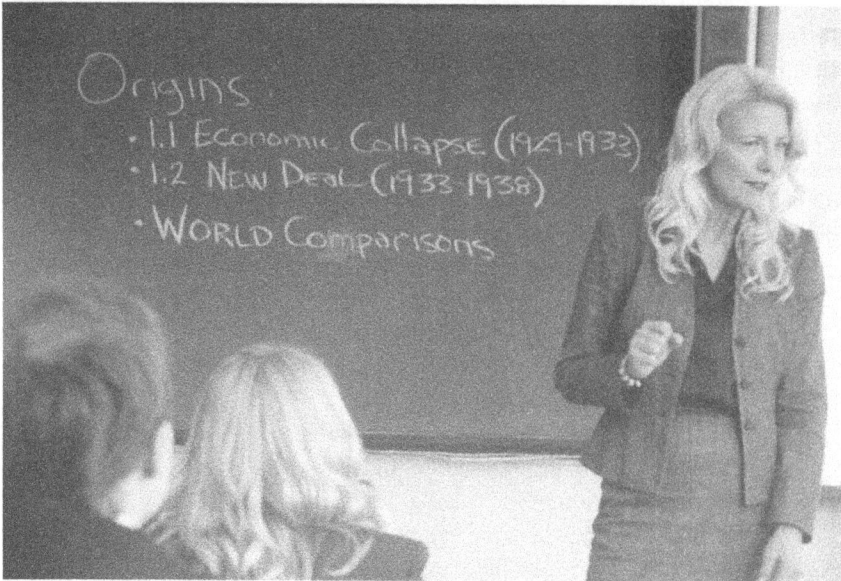

Figure 6.4. Ms. Wilson continuing to assail Nicky over Henry's remarks.

are unfalteringly honest protectors of public safety, *Blue Bloods* indicates that police officers should be able to use torture when they perceive exigent circumstances ("Pilot" 2009). Consonant with this view, Dirty Harry uses torture (in *Dirty Harry*) in a failed effort to save a girl.

While *Blue Bloods* indicates that critiques of the NYPD are misplaced and politically motivated, the Netflix documentary *Making a Murderer* (2015) purports to show an instance where a police department horribly victimizes an innocent man—Steven Avery. Avery is railroaded in 1985 for sexual assault and attempted murder. The documentary creators outline how the police officer who initially took the report of the crime pointed the victim to Avery. The prosecutor proceeds with the case against him in spite of the fact that upward of 20 witnesses serve as alibis—other exculpatory evidence is a time-stamped receipt supporting Avery's claim that he was nowhere near the crime scene at the time of the incident. Avery is convicted and sentenced to over 30 years in prison. During his time in prison the local police (including the sheriff) is apprised of evidence that someone else committed the crime that Avery was convicted of—a someone that at the time of the crime the local police identified as a dangerous sexual predator in the area (and who turns out to be the actual culprit). This evidence is ignored by the police. Ultimately, Avery is exonerated by DNA evidence after 18 years in prison.

After his release Avery pursues a civil lawsuit against the police officials who engineered his conviction. The documentary suggests that the police actions against Avery were so egregious that the county's insurers were refusing to indemnify police officials ("Turning the Tables"). As Avery's civil case is proceeding, a woman who was last seen on Avery's property is murdered, and suspicion falls on Avery. Once Avery officially becomes a person of interest in the woman's murder, the local police are ordered not to participate in the investigation—as their relationship with Avery is deemed to be too tainted. Nevertheless, local police officers (ones Avery was suing) continue to participate in the police investigation, and they plant incriminating evidence in Avery's bedroom (bloody car keys) ("Testing the Evidence")—something the prosecutor virtually concedes in his closing statement to the jury ("The Great Burden"). Avery's nephew (who is mentally impaired) is coerced by police into confessing that he helped his uncle kill the woman. Avery and his nephew are convicted and are currently in prison.

It is with such cases as Steven Avery's where we can see the clear difference between the *Dirty Harry* franchise and *Blue Bloods*. *Blue Bloods* is concerned with the reputation of the NYPD. Harry is only concerned with justice. Thus, in *The Enforcer*, when the police hierarchy zeroes in on an African American nationalist group as the perpetrators of the crime animating the plot Harry disagrees—feeling that the evidence doesn't support this conclusion. While subsequent events expose the actual perpetrators, the situation presents itself in *The Enforcer* where the police leadership is effectively implicated in seeking to railroad innocent men. That would seemingly be a plot that *Blue Bloods* would never replicate—as Frank Reagan (as police commissioner) is cast as a paragon of virtue.

In contrast to *Blue Bloods, NYPD Blue* (1993–2005) is ostensibly more sensitive to the idea that the law and justice are frequently incongruent. This comes into sharp relief with the introduction of Lieutenant Thomas Bale, the new commanding officer of the 15th Precinct. Bale is a by-the-book law enforcement official. He comes into conflict with his detectives when he is first introduced in "Dress for Success" (2004), where he declares that the detective squad of the precinct is widely considered to be "rogue" because they apply their views of justice to help people instead of strictly abiding by the law. Bale explains to the entire squad that his role is to ensure that all detectives strictly adhere to the rules of law enforcement. After several episodes of dealing with cases, Bale comes to the view that helping people who deserve it (i.e., justice) should take precedence over the letter of the law. Bale is particularly affected when one of the detectives he oversees, Sipowicz, has evidence pointing to the fact that he is gay ("Bale Out" 2004). Sipowicz, in spite of his conflictive relationship with the lieutenant and the rules of police procedure, does not log in this evidence (a credit card belonging to Bale was in the possession of someone who robbed gay men), as it had no bearing whatsoever on the outcome of the case at hand—a murder investigation. Sipowicz discreetly gives the card to Bale and tells Bale that the matter will never be spoken of again. In the end, Sipowicz is very disappointed/upset when Bale decides to retire. Bale, for his part, uses his influence to have Sipowicz promoted to the position of commanding officer for the 15th Precinct.

Bonanza (1959–1973), in my estimation, does the best job in all of U.S. television of artistically/poetically conveying criminal justice as a spirit, and not a function of the law, per se. As a long-running Western, *Bonanza* would frequently treat matters involving crime and law enforcement. Pointing to the idea that legal proceedings are in fact political processes is the following quote from the episode "The Spitfire" (1961): "There's a law for you'uns and a law for we'uns, but it ain't the same law." The matriarch of a poor, itinerant family doesn't trust that her son will receive a fair trial involving a killing. Ben Cartwright, acknowledging the validity of her concerns, tells her that he will use his considerable influence to ensure that her son is justly treated. Again indicating that criminal proceedings are a balance of political forces between those that want retribution and those that want fairness for suspects, in "The Initiation" (1972) a young man (played by Ron Howard) who has no family is convinced that he will fall victim to the desire for vengeance if his role in the accidental death of a boy were exposed. He exclaims "I have no people behind me!" His fears are confirmed when an itinerant man is found with the dead boy's horse. The man is on the cusp of being convicted and sent to the gallows when witnesses come forward to tell what actually happened—the boy's heart just stopped in the midst of an innocent initiation ritual overseen by the character played by Ron Howard. In the end, it's only Ben Cartwright's personal intervention that prevents Ron Howard's character from being killed by a mob led by the dead boy's father. The episode "The Desperado" (1971) invokes that reality that the politics of the 19th prevented African Americans from being treated fairly. An African American man is wanted for killing a white man in self-defense. Not even the Cartwrights can help him. He is killed by law enforcement.

"The Measure of a Man" (1989), a *Star Trek: Next Generation* episode, lucidly describes judicial proceedings as a dialectical process—ideally composed of countervailing forces—driving toward the truth. As part of a trial convened to determine Lt. Cmdr. Data's rights as an android, Captain Picard declares "The courtroom is a crucible. In it we burn away irrelevancies until we are left with a pure product, the truth for all time." As suggested by *Making a Murderer*, however, a jury's deference to police and prosecutors may preclude just verdicts even if the truth is made evident.

Significantly, *Blue Bloods* expressly rejects a dialectical understanding of criminal justice when Frank Reagan declares "when it comes to keeping people safe, there's no place for politics." He expresses this view in the episode "Help Me Help You" (2016). Arguably, in this episode Frank takes an antidemocratic stance. The storyline involving Frank centers on the NYPD's "broken windows" policy—which is actual policy. (*Blue Bloods* was also a defender of the NYPD's "stop and frisk" policy ["Ties that Bind" 2013].) Advocates of the broken windows theory of law enforcement hold that all laws must be strictly enforced, as the breaking of even trivial laws contributes to overall lawlessness. In the episode it is acknowledged that minority communities are where the broken windows policy is having the most significant effect—with most seemingly trivial criminal charges imposed upon residents in these neighborhoods. In "Help Me Help You" elected representatives from minority areas object to the NYPD's policy—arguing that minority residents are being tagged with criminal records for small, nuisance infractions of the law. Frank holds that the broken windows program is good for minority communities, as it improves quality of life. Thus, Frank (an unelected official) claims to have a better understanding of the community's needs than elected officials.

CONCLUSION

Blue Bloods posits a skewed understanding of justice as tied to the New York City Police Department. As such, the series in key instances comes across as propaganda for this very institution. Part of this propaganda effort is to expressly hold that criticisms of the NYPD are rooted in (extremist) ideology, not facts. Additionally, that putatively zealous efforts at oversight of the NYPD are not needed, and unnecessarily impugn an outstanding institution as well as those beacons of virtue that serve within it. *Blue Bloods* goes as far as to assert that the NYPD police commissioner has a superior understanding of the community's needs than elected officials.

Making of a Murder (a documentary) directly challenges these suppositions by highlighting the case of Steven Avery—who was victimized at least once by the police (serving 18 years in prison directly due to police malfeasance). While *Blue Bloods* focuses on vaunting the police and smearing its supposed enemies, *NYPD Blue* and *Bonanza* are more centered on the idea of justice (as spirit) being the result of a dialectical process, whereby those voices for law, order and punishment are countervailed by concerns for fairness and humaneness. *NYPD Blue* and *Bonanza* qualify as political art. *Making a Murderer*, in particular, shows that law enforcement officials (and not the law itself) are arguably the prime factors that determine whether or not justice prevails.

The Dirty Harry movie franchise is a significant case because like *Blue Bloods* it is deemed politically conservative popular culture. Employing a dialectical understanding of justice, however, we can see that the Dirty Harry character is not propaganda—unlike *Blue Bloods*. The original *Dirty Harry* did make an argument consonant with conservative reasoning—namely, that the rules of evidence, etc. were too skewed toward protecting the rights of criminal suspects. While one may disagree with such a conclusion, one could reasonably hold such a position. In *Magnum Force* Dirty Harry stands in defense of the rules of evidence and the criminal justice system (more broadly) when he comes into direct conflict with rogue police officers who are murdering those they believe are criminals. *The Enforcer* has Harry getting suspended because he overtly rejects what he thinks is the railroading of innocent men. Thus, in Dirty Harry we see a character engaged in the spirit of justice—fighting for victims as well as those wrongly accused and against those who come down too decisively in punishing perceived criminals.

NOTES

1. Joe Street, *Dirty Harry's America: Clint Eastwood, Harry Callahan, and the Conservative Backlash* (Gainesville: University of Florida Press, 2016), 4.
2. Jacques Rancière, *Aesthetics and Its Discontents*, trans. Steve Corcoran (Malden, MA: Polity, 2009).
3. Marc Redfield, *The Politics of Aesthetics: Nationalism, Gender, Romanticism* (Stanford, CA: Stanford University Press, 2003), 2–3.

4. Donald Phillip Verene, *Hegel's Absolute: An Introduction to Reading the Phenomenology of Spirit* (Albany: State University New York Press, 2007); Stephen Houlgate, *Hegel's 'Phenomenology of Spirit': A Reader's Guide* (New York: Bloomsbury Academic, 2013); James Kreines, *Reason in the World: Hegel's Metaphysics and its Philosophical Appeal* (New York: Oxford University Press, 2015); Andrew Feenberg, *Technosystem: The Social Life of Reason* (Cambridge, MA: Harvard University Press, 2017).

5. Sidney M. Milkis, *Theodore Roosevelt, the Progressive Party, and the Transformation of American Democracy* (Lawrence: University of Kansas Press, 2009); Michael Wolraich, *Unreasonable Men: Theodore Roosevelt and the Republican Rebels Who Created Progressive Politics* (New York, St. Martin's Press 2014).

Chapter Seven

Nazi Takeover of America
The Man in the High Castle
and Star Trek

Amazon Prime recently released the first season of *The Man in the High Castle*. The premise of the series (2015–present) is that it is 1962 in a United States that was conquered by the Nazis and Japanese as a result of World War II. Significantly, this is not the first portrayal in post-9/11 popular culture of a Nazi takeover of the United States. The *Star Trek: Enterprise* (2001–2005) episode "Stormfront" (2004) conveys a fictional reality where the Nazis control much of the Northeast United States, including New York City and Washington, DC. The fictionalization of the Nazis (and Imperial Japan) controlling the United States suggests three key factors: 1.) viewers can accept the fact that Nazism has been imposed on the United States, nevertheless, such an ideology is exogenous to America; 2.) it suggests that the sacrifice the United States made in fighting World War II as well as the Cold War was for naught; and 3.) *the state within the state* arrangement (whereby government authority is invested in secret, non-accountable elements) is inherently an authoritarian, dangerous political arrangement.

A NAZI TAKEOVER OF AMERICA'S GOVERNMENT

Particularly in the aftermath of the U.S. invasion of Iraq, pundits and commentators began alleging that a coterie of right-wing extremists (broadly known as neoconservatives[1]) had hijacked (overtaken) the executive branch. The specific allegation was that a group of unelected policy elites with an aggressive, belligerent global agenda have come to control the American foreign policy apparatus.[2]

In 2002 as the neoconservative agenda (i.e., invading Iraq) is gaining momentum both through the Bush government and the national media—most prominently the *New York Times*[3]—the *Enterprise* episode "Fallen Hero" aired. The Enterprise picks up the Vulcan ambassador to the planet of Mazar—she has been recalled by the her government. Soon after the Enterprise departs, the Mazar government demands that the Vulcan Ambassador (V'lar) return—sending ships in pursuit. After initially refusing to tell Enterprise Captain Jonathan Archer the cause of the current controversy, V'lar relents and informs the Captain why the Mazarites are so eager for her return.

> The Mazarites pursuing us are criminals. They are members of an organization that's infiltrated all levels of government, making themselves wealthy and powerful at the expense of many innocent victims. Their methods include eliminating anyone who stands in their way.

She adds that "the corruption ran deeper than I thought." *The Man in the High Castle* makes direct reference to the American invasion/conquest of Iraq when a Nazi bounty hunter invokes a *most wanted* deck of cards. He murders someone on one of these cards and publicly displays the body—allowing birds to feed on the corpse ("The Illustrated Woman," 2015).

Whether or not "Fallen Hero" is an apt metaphor for the politics that resulted in the U.S. invasion of Iraq (and there is strong evidence that it is[4]), the series *The Man in the High Castle* and the *Enterprise* episode "Stormfront" appear to tap into the reality that at least significant segments of the U.S. populace do not support the military adventurism of the Bush/Obama administrations, and the feeling that these policies are imposed on the public rather than a product of genuine public sentiment. The most significant manifestation of the American public's unsupportive attitude toward U.S. military policies abroad is the public's strong opposition to a military draft.[5] From the perspective of those who oppose such policies as the invasion of Iraq and the torture tactics associated with such policies, the American government is behaving like a modern-day Nazi, or imperial Japanese, regime. "Stormfront" and *The Man in the High Castle* fictionalize this reasoning.

The 2004 *Enterprise* episode "Stormfront" sends Captain Archer back to the World War II period. History has been altered. Time-traveling aliens are aiding the Nazis. The Nazis control much of the Northeast U.S., including New York City and Washington, D.C. Nazis occupy and operate from the White House: "We are inside the home of a former American President. It seems to me your war effort is going well enough." In *The Man in the High Castle* the Germans and Japanese have divided the U.S.—with the Nazis controlling that half east of the Rocky Mountains (renamed the Greater Nazi Reich) and the Japanese that part west of these mountains (designated the Japanese Pacific States) (the Rocky Mountains are a "neutral zone" and lawless). The Nazis in both "Stormfront" and *High Castle* engage in torture. This parallels U.S. torture policies beginning with the invasion of Afghanistan.

The Bush administration in 2001 declares the "War on Terror," and as part of this war orders the invasion of Afghanistan—where Al-Qaeda is head-quartered. As the United States is taking prisoners in Afghanistan, the Bush administration designates many of them to be "enemy combatants"—there-fore denying them Geneva Convention protections, including the prohibition against torturing prisoners of war.[6] The United States opens the Guantanamo prison camp in 2002 to house these so-called enemy combatants—where "ag-gressive interrogation" (i.e., torture techniques) against these prisoners was authorized.[7] The movie *Zero Dark Thirty* (2012) (made in close collaboration with the U.S. military and the Central Intelligence Agency) indicates that torture is used by the U.S. government in its dealings abroad.[8] Additionally, in 2013 the *New York Times* reported that "A nonpartisan, independent re-view of interrogation and detention programs in the years after the Sept. 11, 2001, terrorist attacks concludes that 'it is indisputable that the United States engaged in the practice of torture' and that the nation's highest officials bore ultimate responsibility for it."[9]

The *Enterprise* episode "Anomaly" aired September 2003 and offers a sto-ryline whereby torture is needed to protect Earth from attack. This paralleled Bush administration arguments at the time that "enhanced interrogation" techniques were required to protect the United States from further attack.[10] Shortly after entering the Delphic Expanse to stop the planned destruction of Earth, the Enterprise's fuel stock is pirated: "They took every one of our antimatter storage pods." Without these pods, Enterprise will run out of fuel in a month—"tops." In the raid against Enterprise one of the pirates is cap-tured. Information from this captive (Orgoth) is the only way that Enterprise can retrieve its much-needed fuel. Archer tries to intimidate Orgoth into cooperating, but Orgoth holds that "I don't think you'd be very comfortable torturing another man. You and your crewmates are far too civilized for that. Too moral." Captain Archer tells him otherwise: "I need what was stolen from me. There's too much at stake to let my morality get in the way." Or-goth: "Are you taking me to your torture chamber?" Archer puts Orgoth in an "airlock"—which Archer uses to suffocate Orgoth. Orgoth relents and tells the Captain what he wants to know. Enterprise recovers its much needed fuel. The use of suffocation as a torture technique by *Enterprise* is significant in that the most prominent torture technique deployed by the Bush administra-tion was "waterboarding"—whereby victims feel as if they are suffocating through simulated drowning.[11]

The Man in the High Castle casts torture as a tool used to intimidate and punish political opponents. Torture is standard Nazi and Imperial Japanese policy, used against those who run afoul of either regime. Political opponents are referred to as "Semites"—a racial slur. The viewer is shown instances of people tortured for purposes of maintaining order. To fully understand the use of torture, the idea of *intersubjective agreement* must be taken into account.

American philosopher Richard Rorty, writing in the early 1980s, in fashioning *neopragmatism*, argues that societies are based on *intersubjective agreement*.[12] Thus, what is required for societal stability is enough consensus on a set of ideas—any set of ideas. Hence, what matters is consensus, and not the ideas themselves. Presumably, when there is not enough intersubjective consensus/agreement, then social/political breakdown occurs.

As noted above, over 10 years before Rorty published his path-breaking notion of *intersubjective agreement* the Star Trek episode "Mirror, Mirror" (1967) aired. This original series episode aptly presages Rorty's reasoning— again, explained above. With the *neopragmatism* conceptualization of society as little more than *intersubjective agreement*, the prime goal of institutions is achieving societal cohesion by fashioning, fostering, and/or imposing such agreement. Therefore, authoritarian (dictatorial) regimes, as well as torture practices/technologies, can be effective (even appropriate) means to maintain (impose) *intersubjective agreement*—thereby establishing political/social stability.

One important conclusion from Star Trek's treatment of the *intersubjective agreement* argument is those societies that prioritize achieving such agreement, as opposed to those that base their cohesion on the attainment of justice and democracy, develop/deploy technologies intended to impose political consensus—or, at least, to suppress/punish those that would challenge this consensus. In the Empire (of "Mirror, Mirror" and later "In a Mirror, Darkly" [2005—*Enterprise*]) torture technologies called an "agoniser" and an "agony chamber" exist. The agony chamber is also depicted in *Star Trek: Discovery* (2017–present), when the Discovery visits the Empire universe ("Vaulting Ambition" and "What's Past Is Prologue"—both 2018). When used they cause extreme pain without causing tissue damage. In "In a Mirror, Darkly" the following is explained of the "agony booth": "Traditional forms of punishment can overwhelm the nervous system. After a time, the brain ceases to feel anything." "These sensors continually shift the stimulation from one nerve cluster to another, keeping the subject in a constant state of agony." Thus, pain can endlessly be inflicted. Such fictional technologies presage the 2003 Bush administration's notorious memo authorizing torture. In this memo perpetual, intense pain was deemed legally allowable. Only "death, organ failure or permanent damage resulting in a loss of significant body functions will likely result" were prohibited.[13] While the Bush administration didn't develop infinite pain machines (i.e., agonisers or agony chambers) (as far as we know), technologies/practices like "waterboarding" (where drowning is simulated) were used hundreds of times on individual victims.[14]

It is through such means that the Empire (in "Mirror, Mirror") maintains stability—most importantly, threatens/menaces those that seek to operate outside of (or challenge) its *intersubjective agreement* regime. Communicating the political theory at the heart of the Empire, Spock explains that "Terror must be maintained or the Empire is doomed. It is the logic of history."

The original series episode "Cloud Minders"(1969) depicts a society (the planet of Ardana) where torture technology ("the rays")—and unsurprisingly racism—are used to maintain/stabilize a caste system. (Ardana is a seeming stand-in for South Africa.) In effective imagery the political/economic/social realities of the planet are portrayed—with the privileged/governing caste living a life of aesthetic splendor in a "cloud city" ("Stratos") floating in the heavens; on the (barren) planet surface are where the laboring classes (referred to as "Troglytes") live—working the mines (extracting "zenite"). The residents of Stratos are fair-skinned and fair-haired and partake in the high arts. The Troglytes are dark-haired, dark-skinned, and unwashed.

"The rays" are deployed in an effort to break a political movement in opposition to the governing regime, defying society's *intersubjective agreement*. A prisoner is pressed to provide the names of the putative leaders of the mining caste's rebellion: "You still refuse to disclose the names of the other Disrupters." "There are no Disrupters!" "Very well, if you prefer the rays." She screams in agony, discomforting onlookers. Spock, in his famous calm, equanimous voice, observes that "Violence in reality is quite different from theory."

> But what else can [Troglytes] understand, Mister Spock?
>
> All the little things you and I understand and expect from life, such as equality, kindness, justice.
>
> Troglytes are not like Stratos dwellers, Mister Spock. They're a conglomerate of inferior species.

The use of the threat of torture (and worse) to politically cow a populace is dramatically depicted in the *Next Generation* episode "Face of the Enemy" (1993). Enterprise's ship counselor, Deanna Troi, is impressed into impersonating an officer from the Romulan secret police—known as the "Tal Shiar." Troi is forced into a mission whereby as this officer (named "Major Rakal") she is to oversee the transport of special cargo to the Federation. As a Tal Shiar officer, Troi is able to order a Romulan ship captain into transporting this secret shipment—high-ranking members of the Romulan government who wish to defect. They are in boxes—suspended in "stasis."

Troi, at first, is disoriented and frightened—as she was drugged; kidnaped; surgically altered (without her knowledge); and literally thrust into the role of a Tal Shiar officer abroad an enemy military ship. (If Troi were to be found out she "will be killed.") Troi, however, has empathic abilities (she is able to sense the emotions of others), and she quickly realizes that the Romulans on the ship are petrified of her—a Tal Shiar officer. ("They're all terrified of me.") Her Romulan collaborator explains to Troi: "The purpose of the Tal Shiar is to ensure loyalty [i.e., subservience to the Romulan *intersubjective agreement*]. To defy them is to invite imprisonment . . . or death." We learn that the Romulan government maintains a regime of terror to maintain political stability as "thousands of dissidents [i.e., those who challenge their society's *intersubjective agreement*] . . . live in fear of their lives." When Major Rakal (Troi) decides to take command of the ship, she threatens the bridge crew and their families: "If any one of you defies the Tal Shiar, you will not bear the punishment alone. Your families . . . all of them, will be there beside you." They dutifully accede to her orders.

Troi, as Major Rakal, and the Romulan ship captain (Toreth) engage in an exchange that sums up the difference between a regime based on *intersubjective agreement* and one based on justice. The captain openly resents the Tar Shiar and their crushing of dissent: recounting how it *disappeared* her father for ostensibly questioning the hegemonic *intersubjective agreement*. ("Was the Empire threatened by the words of an old man, a devoted citizen who merely tried to speak his mind?" "He was just an idealistic old man . . . and I never saw him again.") Having lost all patience, Major Rakal barks "*I don't need your devotion, Commander. Just your obedience.*" Toreth retorts: "*That is all you have.*" Thus, regimes predicated on maintaining *intersubjective agreement* compel (force) loyalty, compliance, and subservience. Whereas regimes based on *justice* impel (inspire) sacrifice, service, and commitment.

The Nazis/Japanese do not solely rely on torture to maintain stability in *The Man in the High Castle*. They also use propaganda. Viewers are shown a political advertisement encouraging residents of occupied America to be pragmatic. They should focus on the fact that they have jobs and that they are contributing to a "strong" (i.e., stable) nation.

Star Trek, in the original series episode "Bread and Circuses" (1968), is ostensibly critical of *pragmatism* and its overriding emphasis on societal stability—with the outcome being the persistence of slavery worldwide. Harvard historian Louis Menand points out that the core of *pragmatism* is "the belief that ideas [ethics, morality] should never become ideologies"—which early pragmatists saw as the cause of the American Civil War.[15] Therefore, pragmatists seemingly hold that concepts of justice or political principles should not precede the goal of maintaining social stability. To do so invites devastating conflict (e.g., the American Civil War) and chaos. The Enterprise crew, in "Bread and Circuses," comes upon a planet that is virtually identical to mid-20th Earth (America); except on this world the Roman Empire never collapsed and, instead, spans the entire planet. "A world ruled by emperors who can trace their line back 2,000 years to their own Julius and Augustus Caesars." The result is that slavery continues—in part because the slave system was reformed to maintain its stability: "Long ago, there were [slave] rebellions" but "with each century, the slaves acquired more rights under the law. They received rights to medicine, the right to government payments in their old age, and they slowly learned to be content." Spock: "Slavery evolv- ing into an institution with guaranteed medical payments, old-age pensions." In defending this society, one of the characters explains: "This is an ordered world, a conservative world based on time-honored Roman strengths and vir- tues. . . . There's been no war here for over 400 years." "Could your land of that same era make that same boast?," he asks of the Enterprise landing party (specifically Kirk and McCoy). Explaining why Federation citizens who had come upon this Rome-like world could not be allowed to leave (thereby having the opportunity to tell others of its existence): "I think you can see why they don't want to have their *stability* contaminated by dangerous ideas of other ways and places"—such as *ideologies* of freedom, democracy, and equality—that could be politically destabilizing. Spock, in response, opines: "given a conservative empire, quite understandable."

With the United States ostensibly operating as a traditional, conservative empire, a seeming pessimism has set in. This pessimism is manifest in the series *The Man in the High Castle*.

THE POLITICS OF PESSIMISM

The Man in the High Castle and "Stormfront" both convey a pessimism on the current state of world affairs. This suggests that the optimism ("the end of history") of the victories over Nazism and Stalinist Russia has been lost. In the 1987 pilot episode of *Star Trek: The Next Generation* ("Encounter at Far- point") the argument is explicitly made that the barbarism in human history is over. The all-powerful entity "Q" wearing a 1950s-era U.S. military uniform: "You must return to your world and put an end to the commies. All it takes is a few good men." Captain Picard: "That nonsense is centuries behind us." Later in the episode, before a court convened by Q, Captain Picard proclaims: "We agree there is evidence to support the court's contention that humans have been murderous and dangerous. I say 'have been.'" In the 1987 episode "Lonely Among Us" Picard again suggests that the Cold War was "nonsense" (well in the past): "Do you understand the basis of all that *nonsense* between them?" Riker: "No sir. I didn't understand that kind of hostility even when I studied Earth history." Picard: "Oh? Well, yes, but these life-forms feel such passionate hatred over differences in . . . strangely enough, economic systems." Thus, with the end of the Cold War humanity can expect a future of peaceful coexistence and humaneness.

The Man in the High Castle makes a number of references to American lives lost fighting the Nazis and the Japanese. One of the main characters (Juliana) had her father killed in the Pacific theater. A member of the resistence discusses in graphic terms how his comrades were killed fighting the Nazis. With the complete defeat of the United States, these sacrifices are in vain. *The Man in the High Castle* is more pessimistic than "Stormfront"—as the *Enterprise* episode indicates in the denouement that the Americans are organizing a counteroffensive that will expel the Nazis from North America. Thus, "Stormfront" is more in the way of warning, whereas *The Man in the High Castle* suggests that World War II was fought for no purpose, as wars of territorial conquest, torture, authoritarianism are the norm today, as they were during the Nazi period.

Star Trek, the original series, issues strong warnings against Nazism. "Patterns of Force" (1968), portrays a Nazi regime on the planet of Ekos—which was instituted/sponsored/overseen by a Federation official. With Nazism as the political basis of Ekos, the Ekosians organize around the vilification of Zeons—a population from the neighboring planet of Zeon. ("Why do the Nazis hate Zeons?" "Because without us to hate, there'd be nothing to hold them together. So the Party has built us into a threat, a disease to be wiped out.") In addition to massacring the Zeons on Ekos ("The eliminations have started. Within an hour, the Zeon blight will forever be removed from Ekos"), the Nazi regime organizes a planned genocide (their "Final Solution") against Zeons on their home planet: "Our entire solar system will forever be rid of the disease that was Zeon." *The Man in the High Castle* describes how upon a Nazi takeover of New York City Jews were hanged en masse.

In "City on the Edge of Forever" (1967) one of the Enterprise's crew members (Doctor McCoy) inadvertently goes back in time and prevents the U.S. entrance into World War II. The result is that the Nazis win the war, which subsequently prevents the formation of the Federation and even apparently stops humanity from ever being a spacefaring race. ("Your vessel, your beginning, all that you knew is gone.") Significantly, a factor that allows the Nazis to win is that they perfected the atomic bomb: they "develop the A-bomb first." *The Man in the High Castle* offers the same reason for a Nazi victory—the audience is told they "flattened" Washington DC with a nuclear weapon. The seeming insinuation is that the likes of Nazis can only triumph (broadly speaking) through advanced technology/(super) weaponry—ostensibly implying the inherently limited popularity, appeal of the politics of hate.

AUTHORITARIANISM

With a total Nazi/Japanese victory in *The Man in the High Castle*, authoritarianism is firmly entrenched. Today, authoritarianism is manifest as "the state within the state" (aka the "deep state") phenomenon. The U.S. foreign policy apparatus is the most insulated aspect of government—operating under a veil of secrecy (and misinformation [e.g., Iraq's WMDs]).[16] President Donald J. Trump recently complained that the U.S. *deep state* (within the American intelligence agencies/military) is actively undermining his presidency.[17] *Star Trek: Deep Space Nine* specifically posits that *a state within the state* is a common practice throughout the world system. For the Federation, the state within the state is Section 31.

SECTION 31

Deep Space Nine introduces "Section 31"—a secret intelligence agency that is outside the law. It is described in the following terms: "We don't submit reports or ask for approval for specific operations, if that's what you mean. We're an autonomous department." In another instance, Section 31 is cast as "judge, jury and executioner." Section 31 justifies its existence and means in terms consonant with national security: "We deal with threats to the Federation that jeopardize its very survival." "If you knew how many lives we've saved, I think you'd agree that the ends do justify the means."[18]

Section 31 operatives have no scruples. Prior to the advent of open hostilities between the Dominion and the Federation it infects the Changeling Odo (Chief of Security for *Deep Space Nine*) with a deadly disease in the hopes that he will infect the other Changelings (i.e., the Founders—the leadership caste of the Dominion).[19] (While Odo is a Changeling like the Founders, he rejects the Dominion and allies himself with the Federation.) Section 31 kidnaps a Starfleet officer (Julian Bashir—Chief Medical officer of Deep Space Nine); tortures him (through sleep deprivation); and psychologically disorients him into believing he is a Dominion spy. When Bashir states in disbelief: "Is it possible that the Federation would condone this kind of activity?" A Deep Space Nine crew member cynically responds: "I find it hard to believe that they wouldn't. Every other great power has a unit like Section Thirty-One"[20]—an all-powerful, lawless secret security organization. The 2013 Star

Trek movie *Into Darkness* has Section 31 conduct a false-flag operation to initiate war with the Klingons.

We learn that the Cardassians also operate a secret, autonomous intelligence service—the Obsidian Order. "In theory" the Obsidian Order "answer[s] to the political authority . . . , just as the military does. In practice we both run our own affairs."[21] Later, it is discovered that the Cardassian Obsidan Order and the Romulan Tal Shiar (another intelligence agency) secretly constructed a fleet of military ships, and unilaterally undertake an attack on the Dominion home world. ("If you attack the Dominion . . . You'll be taking Romulus and Cardassia into war.")[22]

AUTHORITARIANISM AS A
THREAT TO HUMAN CIVILIZATION

Arguably, the most extreme and dangerous/destructive example of militarism/authoritarianism in human history is that of the German Nazi regime. Star Trek warns that Nazism and fascism pose profound threats for humanity and civilization.

In *Star Trek: Voyager* "The Killing Game" (1998) a German Nazi officer emphasizes the putative greatness of Germany's past to justify its push for worldwide conquest:

> He's never embraced the Fuhrer or his vision. One does not co-operate with decadent forms of life, one hunts them down and eliminates them. The Kommandant speaks of civilization. The ancient Romans were civilised. The Jews are civilised. But in all its moral decay, Rome fell to the spears of our ancestors as the Jews are falling now. Look at our destiny! The field of red, the purity of German blood. The blazing white circle of the sun that sanctified that blood. No one can deny us, no power on Earth or beyond. Not the Christian Savior, not the God of the Jews. We are driven by the very force that gives life to the universe itself!

The kind of hyper-nationalism advocated by the likes of the Nazis is extremely dangerous in the modern era. Therefore, the parable of the Xindi and the fact that they destroyed their own planet must be taken seriously.

The Xindi are the former inhabitants of the planet Xindi (introduced in *Star Trek: Enterprise*). The Xindi are cleaved into five distinct *civilizations*, with each civilization corresponding to a distinct species: one insectoid, humanoid, aquatic, ape-like, and reptilian. As a result of their competition, the Xindi destroyed their planet: "The war went on for nearly a hundred years. . . . The insectoids and reptilians detonated massive explosions beneath the eight largest seismic fissures. I'd like to think they didn't realize how devastating the result would be."[23]

Much of the intrigue in *The Man in the High Castle* revolves around the fact that the Germans have the atomic bomb, while the Japanese do not. This creates ambitions among certain Nazi political elite to engage in a war with Japan. A high-ranking Nazi decides to pass along atomic weaponry science to the Japanese in the hopes of maintaining a balance of power, thereby avoiding another war. The Japanese high command expresses no desire for a balance of power, but seeks nuclear superiority in order to militarily overtake the Nazis. Just like in the real world, nuclear weapons are an element in great (and not so great) power politics.

With the politics of the state within the state, assassination becomes an effective political tool. Thus, authoritarianism means that political murder is a fact of political life.

THE POLITICS OF ASSASSINATION[24]

Star Trek makes the empirical claim that certain technologies exist in the Empire that do not exist in Federation. As noted above, in the Empire (as conveyed in the series *Enterprise*) exists an agony booth. Notably, when Captain Archer of the Federation feels compelled to torture someone (to save planet Earth) he is forced to use conventional technology (an "airlock") to do so—in the process Archer comes close to killing the person (i.e., the torture victim) who has vital information (*Enterprise*—"Anomaly," 2003).

The *intersubjective agreement* argument in "Mirror, Mirror" is brought into sharper relief in *Deep Space Nine*, where the alternate universe is revisited a century later ("Crossover," 1994). We learn that Kirk's time in the alternate universe had a profound impact. "On my side, Kirk is one of the most famous names in our history." In "Mirror, Mirror" (1967—original series) Kirk apprised Spock of a weapon ("the Tantalus field"). From one's quarters a person could zero in on victims and with the push of a button make them disappear. Kirk counseled Spock to use such technology to profoundly change the Empire, and base it on the values of the Federation. The end result is that the Empire collapses and Earth is occupied.

Focusing on the "Tantalus field," this is explicitly a technology of the Empire—as it does not exist in the Federation universe. The Tantalus field communicates key aspects of the structure and practice of political power in the context of *empire* (i.e., a polity whose priority is the maintenance of *intersubjective agreement*). Importantly, the concept of *intersubjective agreement* does not directly speak to the question of how many people, nor precisely who, has to participate in an *agreement* in order for society to be stable. Authoritarian polities (*empires*) seek to concentrate political and institutional authority in a small number of people—who exercise institutional control and work together to impose their *intersubjective agreement* on the whole of society.

In turn, this is precisely why the phenomenon of *palatial politics* occurs—people maneuver among the coterie of power wielders to hold and/or attain power. In the *Deep Space Nine* episode "When it Rains . . ." (1999) the argument is made that the Klingon Empire's current head of government (Chancellor Gowron) has no significant accomplishments other than successfully mastering Klingon "palace intrigue"[25]: "what has he done except plot and scheme his way to power?"

In a context where political power is highly concentrated, assassination becomes an effective means of advancing a military/political career (agenda)—as rivals/obstacles are vanquished. A plot is afoot during season 1 of *High Castle* to assassinate Hitler because he stands in the way of war against Japan. Allegations that Russian president Vladimir Putin aided in the installation of Donald J. Trump as U.S. President[26] can be interpreted as an effort to politically destroy Trump (i.e., character assassination) and replace his regime with one that is more hostile to Russia.[27] In the Empire universe of "Mirror, Mirror" "Captain Kirk's enemies have a habit of disappearing" (via the Tantalus field). Spock (to Captain Kirk): "I do not intend to simply disappear as so many of your opponents have in the past." As alluded to above, Spock of the Empire uses the Tantalus field to gain the leadership of the Empire, and to fashion a new *intersubjective agreement*. The Klingon Empire's chancellor, K'mpec, is poisoned to open the path to power for an ambitious clan (*Next Generation*—"Reunion" [1990]). In the *Deep Space Nine* episode "Inter Arma Enim Silent Leges" (1999), a clandestine operation is successfully executed to manipulate the politics of the Romulan Star Empire by politically destroying a "Senator" to ensure the appointment of a reliable Federation ally to the Romulan "Continuing Committee"—the highest policymaking body in the Empire. Assassination resulting in the protection/entrenchment of a policy regime brings to mind the President John F. Kennedy assassination, as his killing seemingly cleared the way for a more reliable "Cold War Warrior" in Lyndon B. Johnson to ascend to the American presidency.[28]

CONCLUSION

The Man in the High Castle casts a politics where Nazism/fascism is the dominant global ideology, including in the United States. Significantly, this dominance over the United States in particular comes about—not from its indigenous politics—but through a military conquest of America. A similar scenario is portrayed in the *Star Trek: Enterprise* episode "Stormfront." Both *Star Trek: Enterprise* and *High Castle* give voice to critics who argue that U.S. post-9/11 military and torture policies have been imposed and are not the result of public demands. With militarism and torture becoming the norm in global politics, Star Trek and *High Castle* indicate a demoralization of the current epoch and a broader pessimism that the sacrifices of World War II and the Cold War were for naught. Additionally, *High Castle* and Star Trek of the 1990s and 2000s dramatically portray the authoritarianism that characterize U.S. politics. This politics is executed through *the state within the state* phenomenon—where the national security state is beyond democratic politics. In both *High Castle* and Star Trek such politics are depicted as inherently dangerous and threatening the very survival of the planet in the modern era (i.e., they portend military competition leading to global nuclear war).

NOTES

1. Stefan Halper and Jonathan Clarke, *America Alone: The Neo-Conservatives and the Global Order* (Cambridge: Cambridge University Press, 2004); Justin Vaïsse, *Neoconservatism: The Biography of a Movement* (Cambridge, MA: Harvard University Press, 2010); Jean-François Drolet, *American Neoconservatism: The Politics and Culture of a Reactionary Idealism* (New York: Columbia University Press, 2011).

2. Paul Krugman, "Nonsense and Sensibility," *New York Times*, August 11, 2006, A15; Craig Unger, *The Fall of the House of Bush: The Untold Story of How a Band of True Believers Seized the Executive Branch, Started the Iraq War, and Still Imperils America's Future* (New York: Scribner, 2007).

3. Don Van Natta, Jr., Adam Liptak, and Clifford J. Levy, "The Miller Case: A Notebook, A Cause, a Jail Cell and a Deal," *New York Times*, Oct. 16, 2005, sec. 1, p. 1.

4. George A. Gonzalez, *Energy and the Politics of the North Atlantic* (Albany: State University Press of New York, 2013), chap. 6.

5. Darren K. Carlson, "Public Support for Military Draft Low," Gallup, Nov. 18, 2003. Web; "Military Draft? Polls Finds Americans Opposed," Associated Press, June 24, 2005. Web.

6. "Rewriting the Geneva Conventions," *New York Times*, August 14, 2006, A20.

7. Richard W. Stevenson, "White House says Prisoner Policy Set Humane Tone," *New York Times*, June 23, 2004, A1.

8. Scott Shane, "Portrayal of C.I.A. Torture in Bin Laden Film Reopens a Debate," *New York Times*, Dec. 13, 2012, A1; "About Those Black Sites," *New York Times*, Feb. 18, 2013, A16.

9. Scott Shane, "U.S. Practiced Torture After 9/11, Nonpartisan Review Concludes," *New York Times*, April 16, 2013, A1; also see Mark Mazzetti, "Panel Faults

C.I.A. Over Brutality Toward Terrorism Suspects," *New York Times*, Dec. 10, 2014, A1; "Dark Again After the Torture Report," *New York Times*, Dec. 12, 2014, A34.

10. "Effort to Prohibit Waterboarding Fails in House," Associated Press. March 12, 2008. Web.

11. Scott Shane, "Waterboarding Used 266 Times on 2 Suspects," *New York Times*, April 20, 2009, A1.

12. Richard Rorty, *Philosophy and the Mirror of Nature* (Princeton: Princeton University Press, 1981); Michael Bacon, *Richard Rorty: Pragmatism and Political Liberalism* (Lanham: Lexington Books, 2007); Neil Gross, *Richard Rorty: The Making of an American Philosopher* (Chicago: University of Chicago Press, 2008).

13. As quoted in Mark Mazzetti, "'03 U.S. Memo Approved Harsh Interrogations," *New York Times*, April 2, 2008. Web.

14. Shane, "Waterboarding Used 266 Times on 2 Suspects"; Jonathan Hafetz, "Don't Execute Those We Tortured," *New York Times*, Sept. 25, 2014, A31; Mazzetti, "Panel Faults C.I.A. Over Brutality Toward Terrorism Suspects."

15. Louis Menand, *The Metaphysical Club* (New York: Farrar, Straus, and Giroux, 2001), xii.

16. Terry H. Anderson, *Bush's Wars* (New York: Oxford University Press, 2011); Roger Z. George, and Harvey Rishikoff, *The National Security Enterprise: Navigating the Labyrinth* (Washington D.C.: Georgetown University Press, 2011); John Prados, *The Family Jewels: The CIA, Secrecy, and Presidential Power* (Austin: University of Texas Press, 2013); Mazzetti, "Panel Faults C.I.A. Over Brutality Toward Terrorism Suspects"; Michael P. Colaresi, *Democracy Declassified: The Secrecy Dilemma in National Security* (New York: Oxford University Press, 2014).

17. Julie Hirschfeld Davis, "'Deep State'? Until Now, It Was a Foreign Concept," *New York Times*, March 7, 2017, A19.

18. *Deep Space Nine*—"Inquisition," 1998.

19. *Deep Space Nine*—"Extreme Measures," 1999.

20. *Deep Space Nine*—"Inquisition," 1998.

21. *Deep Space Nine*—"Defiant," 1994.

22. *Deep Space Nine*—"Improbable Cause," 1995.

23. *Enterprise*—"The Shipment," 2003.

24. Benjamin F. Jones and Benjamin A. Olken, "Do Assassins Really Change History?" *New York Times*, April 12, 2015, SR12.

25. In the *Star Trek: Voyager* episode "Author, Author" (2001) Klingon politics are referred to as "palace intrigue".

26. Matt Flegenheimer and Scott Shane, "Bipartisan Voices Back U.S. Agencies on Russia Hacking," *New York Times*, Jan. 6, 2017, A1; Nicholas Fandos and Sharon LaFraniere, "Two Reports on Meddling: Choose Your Own Verdict," *New York Times*, April 28, 2018, A14.

27. "Mr. Trump and Mr. Putin, Best Frenemies," *New York Times*, June 29, 2018, A26; Michelle Goldberg, "Trump Shows The World He's Putin's Lackey," *New York Times*, July 17, 2018, A21; Sheryl Gay Stolberg, Nicholas Fandos, and Thomas

Kaplan, "Measured Condemnation but No G.O.P. Plan to Act," *New York Times*, July 17, 2018, A1.

    28. Robert Dallek, *Lyndon B. Johnson: Portrait of a President* (New York: Oxford University Press, 2005); James N. Giglio, *The Presidency of John F. Kennedy* (Lawrence: University of Kansas Press, 2006); Godfrey Hodgson, *JFK and LBJ: The Last Two Great Presidents* (New Haven: Yale University Press, 2015).

Chapter Eight

Post-9/11 Politics on Television

Veep, House of Cards,
Game of Thrones, **and**
Star Trek: Enterprise

Four television series stand out for their treatment of present-day politics: *Veep, House of Cards, Game of Thrones,* and *Star Trek: Enterprise.* All, in their own way, suggest that American democracy is in deep crisis. *Veep* depicts the personage of the U.S. president as little more than a joke—dominated by an obsession with the media; hopelessly handicapped by special interests; and, ultimately, incapable of accomplishing anything progressive. *House of Cards* indicates that the president should be a murderous sociopath, and in order to domestically accomplish anything notable the executive must act unilaterally—outside of normal "democratic" politics. Perhaps the most intriguing treatments of politics on television post 9/11 are provided by *Game of Thrones* and *Star Trek: Enterprise.* These series replicate neoconservative ideation concerning executive authority and broader politics. Importantly, while replicating neoconservative political ideation, *Game of Thrones* and *Enterprise* provide insight into the explicit dangers of said politics.

DEMOCRACY AS LIABILITY

The opening credits of *Veep* (2012–present) convey an ongoing reality of U.S. politics. Political leaders are almost entirely products of the media and opinion polls on the personal popularity of candidates.[1] The show's opening displays newspaper-style headlines and poll results that describes/outlines Selina Myers's fortunes during the presidential election season that results in her becoming vice president and ultimately president—upon the resignation of the incumbent. Thus, it was Selina's media operations, and the media's treatment of her, that resulted in her ascendancy to the executive branch. What's missing is any policy or political program.

87

Given the outsized role of the media as kingmaker, Myers's advisers be-come little more than consultants on how to manage and maintain a positive image vis-à-vis the media. In this game of media management, average peo-ple are nothing more than political props. Thus, Myers, in spite of running for president, becoming vice president and ultimately president, resides in a co-coon, where the media completely mediates her relationship with the public.

Vice President, and, later, President Myers undertakes political initiatives because she wants to have a positive impact. Put differently, since elections amount to almost entirely personal popularity contests, Myers's policy initia-tives are the result of her own ethics and not the result of electoral politics. Indeed, electoral politics is cast as an obstacle to actually helping people. For reasons that are unexplained, Myers, as President, turns against her own "Families First" proposal—intended to help low-income families. While the precise reasons for Myers lobbying against her own legislation are murky, it is clear that this decision was made with an eye to her effort to get elected as President ("B/ill" 2015). When she is vice president, Myers's clean-energy initiative falls victim to the oil lobby ("Tears" 2012).

Similarly, in *House of Cards* (2013–2018), Congress poses a virtually insu-perable obstacle to addressing the public's needs. At the end of season 2, Frank Underwood becomes president. During season 3 Underwood spearheads a jobs program intended to employ 10 million people. His plan is to divert Social Se-curity and Medicare monies to finance his program. Congress is unwilling to go along, and Underwood misappropriates disaster relief funds to initiate his jobs plan. While the audience may question the justice/ethics of shifting funds away from pensions, health care, and disaster relief for an employment program, it is nevertheless the case that Congress solely plays an obstructionist role—offering no answers whatsoever to confront America's job crisis.[2]

VIOLENCE AND THE PRESIDENCY

Over the course of two seasons Frank Underwood maneuvers himself from a leadership position in the House of Representatives into the White House as president. Like Selina Myers, Underwood becomes president upon the incumbent's resignation. Underwood is driven by overwhelming, unbridled personal ambition. Indeed, in the course of his machinations to become vice president, and then president, Underwood personally murders two people—including throwing a young woman (a former lover) under a moving train.

During season 3 of *House of Cards* Underwood's ability to remorselessly kill people is cast as a virtue, since as president he orders the death of inno-cent children as collateral damage in the course of drone warfare. Certainly

a more scrupulous person would be unable to make such deadly decisions—
not at least without incurring significant psychological stress, even damage.
For instance, a recent *New York Times* report details how the operators of
military drones are resigning at high rates due to the moral/ethical strain
of killing—even though they are separated by thousands of miles from kill
sites.[3] Thus, the U.S. President today, like Frank Underwood, has to be willing and able to murder—without letting moral considerations get into the
way.[4] President Barak Obama directly participated in selecting people for
assassination[5]—whereby in many instances collateral deaths of innocents
occurred.[6]

The necessity of having a president who is willing/able to wantonly kill
is explicitly communicated in "Chapter 36" (2015) of *House of Cards* when
Underwood meets Russian President Viktor Petrov (played by an actor who
is a dead ringer for Vladimir Putin) in a remote, austere military base in the
Middle East. Petrov seemingly tries to intimidate Underwood by recounting how as a soldier in the Soviet-Afghan War he brutally killed someone.
Petrov stares Underwood in the eyes and asks him if he could do the same.
Underwood doesn't flinch—the audience knowing full well that he's more
than capable of doing so. Petrov is somewhat shaken, when after sizing up
Underwood, he sees that Underwood is not someone to trifle with (Petrov
to Underwood: "You're ruthless. Like me."; Underwood: "Sometimes we
must be ruthless with those who hate us."). Therefore, the world is led by
extremely dangerous people, and the U.S. needs someone at the helm that is
able to act in kind.

While *Veep* and *House of Cards* draw upon the lack of faith that the public
has in American political institutions (especially Congress) and elections,[7]
Game of Thrones casts a world where executive authority is absolute and
unquestioned. In doing so it outlines how inherently dangerous is a world
where democratic aspirations are completely absent and all political authority
is vested in a monarch.

POLITICAL STABILITY AND TYRANNY

Game of Thrones (2011–present) is set in a fictional feudal world, where
absolute monarchies are the only form of government. This results in tyranny
and legitimacy crises. These factors work to cause arguably the most significant political murder in all of television history—that of Eddard "Ned" Stark.
In the absence of democracy, or a firm normative core anchoring the politics
of Westeros—the central polity of *Game of Thrones*—its government must
rely on violence/fear to maintain stability. With the maintenance of stability

as the primary focus of King's Landing (the capital of Westeros), Stark falls victim when he seeks to prioritize legality and transparency in government.

King Robert Baratheon offered the clearest political theory underlying the Seven Kingdoms of Westeros during his reign. Baratheon notes that "I've got Seven Kingdoms to rule!" He then rhetorically asks "Do you think it's honor that's keeping the peace?" He answers himself: "It's fear—fear and blood."[8] Mr. Spock, in the Empire universe of the original-series *Star Trek* episode "Mirror, Mirror" (1967), similarly states that "Terror must be maintained or the Empire is doomed. It is the logic of history." Later, King Robert, in explaining why he thinks it is necessary to kill a teenage girl rival to his throne, argues that he cannot inspire the loyalty of the masses and this makes his regime vulnerable to outside attack/invasion: Westeros's political "purpose died with the Mad King." It is this lack of "purpose" that Robert attributes to the corruption at the center of his government: "that's all the realm is now: Back-stabbing and scheming and arse-licking and money-grubbing." He adds "Sometimes I don't know what holds it together."[9]

A profound problem with such a polity—whose purpose is only maintaining stability[10]—is that decision-makers must lack scruples. They must be able to kill, torture, exile, and imprison those who threaten the stability of the kingdom. Therefore, the best prince is a sociopath; one who is able to forgo empathy and not let moral considerations weigh him down.[11]

Alas, no prince, however powerful, governs alone. He must rely on henchmen to carry out his orders, and they, too, must be sociopaths. When King Baratheon asks his Council's opinion on the fate of the pregnant teenage rival (Daenerys), with the exception of Ned Stark, all voice support for her assassination (explicitly citing stability for what they admit is a dastardly act):[12]

> It is a terrible thing we must consider, a vile thing. Yet we who presume to rule must sometimes do vile things for the good of the realm. Should the gods grant Daenerys a son, the realm will bleed.

> I bear this girl no ill will, but should the Dothraki invade, how many innocents will die? How many towns will burn? Is it not wiser, kinder even, that she should die now so that tens of thousands might live? We should have had them both killed years ago.

> When you find yourself in bed with an ugly woman, best close your eyes, get it over with. Cut her throat. Be done with it.

Later, these councillors will betray the King by supporting Cersi against Ned Stark.

Herein lies the corruption of a polity whose only purpose is stability: it essentially must employ murderers in key positions of responsibility. This is where palace politics becomes dangerous and dirty. As those around the king will by necessity be killers and by definition amoral. It is this reality that is the undoing of Ned Stark. Stark may be among the most significant political figures in all of television history. Here is someone who sought to rule through transparency, legality, and ethics (i.e., "honorably"), and was killed because of it.[13]

Why does Ned wish to govern as such? He is not naive nor stupid. He very well understood that in confronting Cersi he couldn't solely rely on King Robert's will and testament. Ned wisely approached Bayliss to ensure that the balance of forces in the King's palace was favorable to him when he declared that he was regent protector and therefore the rightful ruler—at least for the moment. Stark's tactical error was in believing that he could persuade Bayliss to follow the law, and accept the fact that Stannis Baratheon was ultimately the rightful king.

The fundamental problem confronting Ned is his conscience. He understands the brutality at the core of the Westeros political order. Indeed, in the first episode of the series Ned beheads a boy only because he was AWOL from his duties as a ranger. The boy explained that he ran away because of the zombie "White Walkers" he witnessed on the other side of the "wall." While Ned could see that the boy was genuinely frightened and was intrigued by his claims, the law didn't allow for mitigating factors or even temporary reprieves. So Ned brutally killed the boy on the spot. Thus, Ned's conscience was eased only by the fact that the brutality of Westeros was (he believed/hoped) legal, fair (applied equally), and transparent. Such traits, however, are in direct contradiction to a polity predicated on fear/stability—as legality, fairness, and transparency cannot get in the way of the maintenance of fear/stability. In the case of Ned it was his insistence that the law be followed with the ascension of Stannis Barathan—someone that Bayliss viewed as an improper choice for king (since it would likely trigger a civil war). It is this fact that ostensibly prompts Bayliss to betray Ned to Cersi, and, ultimately, leads to Ned's decapitation.

NEOCONSERVATIVE POLITICS

The normative core of *Game of Thrones* is not found in political justice (e.g., democracy, social welfare) but in protection—another vector/iteration of the maintenance of stability. The first scene of the television series depicts White Walkers—zombie-like creatures. Thus, the show begins by foreshadowing a showdown with ghastly beings. Another external threat to the civilized world, Westeros, are the "Wildings"—who like White Walkers lurk in the lands beyond the "Wall" (the northern border of Westeros [i.e., civilization]). Some wildings are cast as cannibals preying on people for their flesh.

While White Walkers and ravenous cannibals are fantasy, *Star Trek: Enterprise* engages in a more subtle use of the "other" to establish sovereignty/ legitimacy. This results in a planetary-wide racist movement. Moreover, Star Trek outlines how security threats can be used to justify dictatorship and torture.

THE "FRIEND/ENEMY" DICHOTOMY AND STAR TREK

Carl Schmitt (1888–1985) is in the pantheon of neoconservative thinkers. Schmitt was an architect of the Nazi Germany legal regime and known as the "Crown Jurist" of the Nazis.[14] He was an ostensive mentor to Leo Strauss (1899–1973), who was a German Jew who immigrated to the United States in 1937 because of the Nazis. (Strauss, in particular, is considered to be a lodestone for American neoconservatives.)[15] Schmitt wrote *The Concept of the Political* in 1929, and Strauss a set of sympathetic "Notes" to Schmitt's book.[16] Schmitt provided a letter of recommendation for Strauss that facilitated Strauss's obtaining an academic position at the University of Chicago.[17]

Schmitt held that at the center of politics is the distinction "between friend and enemy."[18] Social and political cohesion is based on this foe/friend dichotomy. Reflective of Schmitt's "friend/enemy" reasoning, in the *Next Generation* episode "Face of the Enemy" (1993) the point is made that Romulans have an "absolute certainty about . . . who is a friend and who is an enemy." The main component of Hitler's and the Nazis' political/propaganda argumentation was directed at an imaginary coalition of Western bankers and Eastern communists conspiring against Germany. According to Nazi mythology (myopia), Jews were at the center of this worldwide anti-Germany coalition. In the face of this global conspiracy directed against Germany, the Hitler regime argued that the German people must be unified (no dissent whatsoever), and strike back (World War II).[19] In her synthesis of Strauss's writings, Shadia B. Drury renders the following observation: "Like Schmitt, Strauss believes that politics is first and foremost about the distinction between WE and THEY. Strauss thinks that a political order can be stable only if it is united by an external threat."[20]

The *Star Trek* movie *First Contact* (1996) is predicated on a we/they distinction. The action of the movie takes place in the year 2063. The Borg go back in Earth's history to prevent humanity's first contact with the Vulcans. This initial exposure to an alien culture occurs because Zephran Cochrane conducts humanity's first successful warp drive experiment. (Warp speed represents a speed faster than light.) When the Vulcans detect Cochrane's ship achieving warp speed, they decide to introduce themselves to earth-lings—"first contact." In this iteration (*First Contact*) of *Star Trek*'s histo-riography of Earth in 2063 humanity is in what is referred to in the movie script as a "Second Dark Age."[21] What rallies humanity from its disarray is its contact with the Vulcans. Troi states, "It unites humanity in a way no one ever thought possible when they realize they're not alone in the universe."

Therefore, the political foundation of humanity in the mid-twenty-first century is the we/they dichotomy—with the Vulcans serving as "they." "The political enemy is not necessarily morally evil." Instead, Schmitt held that the potential enemy "is merely the other, the stranger, and it is suffi-cient that according to his nature he is in a special intense way existentially something different and alien, so that in the extreme case conflicts with him are possible."[22]

In *Enterprise* conflict with the Vulcans does occur. "The Andorian Incident" (2001) concludes with the exposure of a Vulcan spy station by Captain Archer, which earns the ire of the Vulcans. The Vulcan ambassador to Earth complains "The Andorians wouldn't have found the [spy] station if your people hadn't interfered." The *Enterprise* has "been in space for six months and they've already destabilized an entire sector" ("Shadows of P'Jem" 2002). "Fusion" (2002) involves a set of Vulcans who, contrary to Vulcan norms, embrace their emotions. ("I always knew there had to be more to life than just logic and reason.") One of these Vulcans telepathi-cally "rapes" T'Pol (a Vulcan and *Enterprise's* first officer), and Captain Archer engages in an intense fistfight with the transgressor. The episodes "The Forge" (2004), "Awakening" (2004), and the "Kir'Shara" (2004) make up a story arc whereby Earth's embassy on Vulcan is bombed, kill-ing Admiral Forrest (Archer's mentor), and the *Enterprise* crew gets swept up in internal Vulcan religious and political strife—with an attempt made against Captain Archer's life, and the *Enterprise* and Vulcan military ships coming to a face-off. In the denouement, we learn that elements within the Vulcan government were behind the bombing of the Earth embassy, and that a faction still in the government wants to pull the planet toward a political/military alliance with the Romulans—an intention ominously threatening to Earth.

The we/they or friend/foe dichotomy at the heart of Earth's politics in *En-terprise* and *First Contact* is in sharp contrast to earlier iterations of *Star Trek*, where state-building was accomplished through the progressive expansion of political rights and social justice, like in the American Revolution (original series—"The Omega Glory," 1968), the U.S. Civil War (original series— "The Savage Curtain," 1969), the fight against fascism (original series— "City on the Edge of Forever," 1967), and the Bell Uprising, which takes place in 2024 (*Deep Space Nine*—"Past Tense," 1995). Such an ontology of social/political change through revolutionary moments/events is entirely consistent (if not inspired) by classic Marxism.[23]

It is significant that in *First Contact* (the movie script) by 2063 San Francisco is destroyed.[24] In "Past Tense" (1995—*Deep Space Nine*), San Francisco is where the anti-neoliberal Bell Uprising (the basis of a new global politics) occurs in 2024.

EARTH UNDER ATTACK

The last episode of *Enterprise* season 2 ("The Expanse" 2003) has a terrorist attack committed against Earth—the Florida peninsula. The "probe"—that upon explosion killed 7 million people—was launched from a remote and uncharted area of space known as the Delphic Expanse. The Enterprise crew learns that this probe was only a "test" and a larger explosive is being planned to destroy the entirety of Earth. This attack is being carried out by the "Xindi." Season 3 is dedicated to Enterprise's effort to stop this threat against humanity.

In the aftermath of the 2001 9/11 attack, the Bush administration argued for greater political authority to be vested in the White House—including the power to make war. Using the theory of the Unitary Executive, the Bush White House held that the U.S. Constitution empowered the president to act unilaterally—without consultation or authorization from the legislative or judicial branches of government.[25] Carl Schmitt argued that the executive (the president) under the Weimar constitution had broad discretion to declare a state of emergency—even if only a governing majority could not be established in the Reichstag (parliament). When an effort was made to limit the power of the executive during a "crisis," Schmitt argued against enumerating the executive's powers during such a crisis—thereby standing for open-ended, unfettered executive authority in such circumstances.[26]

In the *Deep Space Nine* episode "Homefront" (1996) a terrorist bombing occurs on Earth, killing 27. In the aftermath of this attack, Starfleet (i.e., the military) argues for greater security measures. The president of Earth resists this suggestion: "I understand the need for increased security, but . . ."

President: I believe the changeling threat is somewhat less serious than Starfleet does.

Admiral Leyton: Mister President, I assure you the threat is real.

President: For all we know, there was only one changeling on Earth, and he may not even be here anymore.

Captain Sisko: But if he is here, we have a problem. There's no telling how much damage one changeling could do.

President: Forgive me for saying so, Captain, but you sound a little . . . paranoid

Sisko: Do I?

This exchange presages the Bush administration contention that the Al-Qaeda threat required greater political/legal latitude for the military-security apparatus. President Bush took this position even though the 9/11 attack involved only a handfull of perpetrators, many of whom died in the attack.

In the end, the Earth president agrees to the enhanced security measures being proposed by the military. Interestingly, the enhanced security measures are seemingly instituted with simply the President's signature—there are no other deliberations presented or discussed.

These increased security measures are cast as necessary defensive measures to protect "paradise" or utopia (i.e., Earth):

I would hate to be remembered as the Federation President who destroyed paradise.

We're not looking to destroy paradise, Mister President. We're looking to save it.

Just like Schmitt held that the executive needed emergency powers to protect the Weimar constitution, the Bush administration argued for enhanced security measures and greater power for the presidency to protect American "freedom and democracy."[27]

In the denouement of "Homefront" Earth experiences a planet-wide blackout. A state of emergency has been declared. The subsequent *Deep Space Nine* episode "Paradise Lost" (1996) begins by showing platoons of troops patrolling the street, and everyone submitting to security screening (blood tests) to establish that they are not enemies. We learn that the power outage was perpetrated by elements within Starfleet. Thus, *Deep Space Nine* issues a caution against the use of national-security threats to suspend civil and political rights, as well as democratic decision-making processes: "What you're trying to do is seize control of Earth and place it under military rule." "If that's what it takes to stop the Dominion."

TERRA PRIME

The *Enterprise* series concludes in 2005 and the penultimate episode centers on the group Terra Prime (episode title). Initially, this organization is described as xenophobic: "They want to stop all contact with alien species." "They believe it's corrupting our way of life." Terra Prime "had a resurgence following the Xindi attack." Later, we learn that Terra Prime is racist: "This is an alien-human hybrid. Living proof of what will happen if we allow ourselves to be submerged in an interstellar coalition. Our genetic heritage . . ." "That child is a cross-breed freak. How many generations before our genome is so diluted that the word 'human' is nothing more than a footnote in some medical text?" The leader of Terra Prime declares "I'm returning Earth to its rightful owners." The group seeks to scuttle the formation of the Federation by promising to destroy Starfleet command (in San Francisco) unless all aliens leave Earth. Referring to signs of popular support for Terra Prime and its agenda, the Vulcan Ambassador Soval notes: "The fact that Paxton has the support of so many of your people is . . . troubling." An Andorian ambassador makes the point that: "Earthmen talk about uniting worlds, but your own planet is deeply divided. Perhaps you're not quite ready to host this conference" promoting interstellar cooperation.

CONCLUSION

Veep, *House of Cards*, *Game of Thrones*, and *Star Trek: Enterprise* suggest that American democracy is in profound crisis. *Veep* is a lighthearted comedy that plays on the public's view of political leaders (institutions) as inept, vacuous, dominated by special interests and short-term political expediency. *House of Cards* makes a more explicit argument for a strong executive in domestic affairs. This is credible in a context where Congress appears to be hopelessly hamstrung. Additionally, *House of Cards* indicates that the president must be free of moral, ethical considerations. This seeming need is required due to the War on Terror, in which serial war and drone assassinations are cast as part of the fact that 9/11 "changed everything." The popularity of *Game of Thrones* suggests that the public is in a post-democracy mood, and views an absolutist executive as a reasonable (if flawed) form of government to maintain stability and defend against external threats.

Arguably, *Star Trek: Enterprise* is a more analytical, thoughtful treatment of the politics of protection—where legitimacy is maintained through the provision of security. In the absence of a well-functioning democracy, political elites emphasize threats (the "other") in order to maintain sovereignty and political stability. With 9/11 serving as perhaps the seminal event in the contemporary period, much of *Enterprise* (2001–2005) was dedicated to depicting a politics where national security is politically predominant. *Enterprise* and Star Trek, more broadly, demonstrate how a political fixation on the "other" and security can/will lead to authoritarianism, torture, and racism.

NOTES

1. Martin P. Wattenberg, *The Rise of Candidate-Centered Politics: Presidential Elections of the 1980s* (Cambridge, MA: Harvard University Press, 1992); Brian Arbour, *Candidate-Centered Campaigns: Political Messages, Winning Personalities, and Personal Appeals* (New York: Palgrave Macmillan, 2014); Kathryn Cramer Brownell, *Showbiz Politics: Hollywood in American Political Life* (Chapel Hill: University of North Carolina Press, 2014).

2. Neil Irwin, "The New Jobs Numbers Are Weaker Than They Look," *New York Times*, July 2, 2015. Web.

3. Christopher Drew and Dave Philipps, "Burnout Forces U.S. to Curtail Drone Flights," *New York Times*, June 17, 2015, A1; also see Pratap Chatterjee, "Our Drone War Burnout," *New York Times*, July 14, 2015, A21.

4. Lloyd C. Gardner, *Killing Machine: The American Presidency in the Age of Drone Warfare* (New York: New Press, 2013).

5. Scott Shane, "A Court to Vet Kill Lists," *New York Times*, Feb. 9, 2013, A1; David Cortright, Rachel Fairhurst, and Kristen Wall, eds., *Drones and the Future of Armed Conflict: Ethical, Legal, and Strategic Implications* (Chicago: University of Chicago Press, 2015).

6. Declan Walsh and Ihsanullan Tipu Mehsud, "Civilian Deaths in Drone Strikes Cited in Report," *New York Times*, Oct. 22, 2013, A1.

7. Zephyr Teachout, *Corruption in America: From Benjamin Franklin's Snuff Box to Citizens United* (Cambridge, MA: Harvard University Press, 2014); Justin Wolfers, "Congress and Us: A Hate-Love Relationship," *New York Times*, June 19, 2014. Web; Lynn Vavreck, "The Long Decline of Trust in Government, and Why That Can Be Patriotic," *New York Times*, July 3, 2015. Web; Eric Lichtblau, "I.R.S. Expected to Stand Aside as Nonprofits Increase Role in 2016 Race," *New York Times*, July 6, 2015, A13; Alan Rappeport and Thomas Kaplan, "A Battle to Protect Proposed Tax Breaks," *New York Times*, September 29, 2017, A16.

8. *Game of Thrones*—"The Wolf and the Lion," 2011.

9. *Game of Thrones*—"The Wolf and the Lion."

10. Richard Tuck, *Hobbes: A Very Short Introduction* (New York: Oxford University Press, 2002); Noel Malcolm, ed., *Thomas Hobbes: Leviathan* (New York: Oxford University Press, 2012 [1668]).

11. Niccolo Machiavelli, *The Prince* (New York: Penguin, 2015 [1532]).

12. *Game of Thrones*—"The Wolf and the Lion."

13. Henry Jacoby, *Game of Thrones and Philosophy: Logic Cuts Deeper Than Swords* (New York: Wiley, 2012); Stephen Benedict Dyson, *Otherworldly Politics: The International Relations of Star Trek, Game of Thrones, and Battlestar Galactica* (Baltimore: Johns Hopkins University Press, 2015).

14. Joseph W. Bendersky, *Carl Schmitt: Theorist for the Reich* (Princeton: Princeton University Press, 1983).

15. Anne Norton, *Leo Strauss and the Politics of American Empire* (New Haven: Yale University Press, 2004); Francis Fukuyama, "After Neoconservatism," *New York Times Magazine*, February 19, 2006, 62.

16. Leo Strauss, "Notes on Carl Schmitt, *The Concept of the Political*," in *The Concept of the Political*, expanded ed., by Carl Schmitt (Chicago: University of Chicago Press, 2007 [1932]).

17. Daniel Tanguay, *Leo Strauss: An Intellectual Biography* (New Haven: Yale University Press, 2007); Steven B. Smith, "Leo Strauss: The Outlines of a Life," in *Cambridge Companion to Leo Strauss*, ed. Steven B. Smith (New York: Cambridge University Press, 2009), 18.

18. "The specific political distinction to which political actions and motives can be reduced is that between friend and enemy." Carl Schmitt, *The Concept of the Political*, expanded ed. (Chicago: University of Chicago Press, 2007 [1929]), 26.

19. Jane Caplan, *Nazi Germany* (New York: Oxford University Press, 2008); Jeffrey Herf, *The Jewish Enemy: Nazi Propaganda during World War II and the Holocaust* (Cambridge, MA: Harvard University Press, 2008).

20. Shadia B. Drury, *Leo Strauss and the American Right* (New York: St. Martin's Press, 1997), 23.

21. The script notes to the movie: "A Third World War. Nuclear explosions, environmental disasters, tens of millions dead. The United States ceases to exist. All political authority vanishes. Humanity teetering on the edge of the Second Dark Age." http://www.st-minutiae.com/academy/literature329/fc.txt

22. Schmitt, *Concept of the Political*, 27.

23. Peter Singer, *Marx: A Very Short Introduction* (New York: Oxford University Press, 2001); Gareth Stedman Jones, *Karl Marx: Greatness and Illusion* (Cambridge, MA: Harvard University Press, 2016).

24. The following is in the 1995 movie script:

Scrimm (2063 resident of Earth): "Where are you from most recently?"

Picard: "California. San Francisco"

Scrimm: "Beautiful city. Used to be, anyway. I didn't think anyone still lived there." http://www.st-minutiae.com/academy/literature329/fc.txt

25. Jonathan Mahler, "After the Imperial Presidency," *New York Times Magazine*, Nov. 9, 2008, MM42; Ryan J. Barilleaux, and Christopher S. Kelley, eds., *The Unitary Executive and the Modern Presidency* (College Station: Texas A&M University Press, 2010).

26. Bendersky, *Carl Schmitt*, chap. 4.

27. "After the Attacks: Bush's Remarks to Cabinet and Advisers," *New York Times*, September 13, 2001. Web; also see Jim Rutenberg and Sheryl Gay Stolberg, "In Prime-Time Address, Bush Says Safety of U.S. Hinges on Iraq," *New York Times*, September 12, 2006. Web.

Conclusion

Art as Knowledge of
Metaphysics and Politics

My argument in this volume is that art (especially popular art) can be an effective, important source of knowledge. This argument is predicated on the idea that normative values are rooted in the Hegelian Absolute. Thus, presumably a key means of comprehending the Absolute is through art. Popular art is important to comprehending the Absolute because creators and audiences often connect through *authentic* political, philosophical motifs. Following from this theory, I have turned to Nazi cinema, the Star Trek (broadcast) franchise, *Veep*, *House of Cards*, *The Man in the High Castle*, and *Game of Thrones* to gain knowledge of the Absolute and the public's perception of how American political elites are operating.

Accepting art as evidence of the Absolute entails a completely different theory of literary criticism from that of deconstructionism (chapter 1). Adherents of deconstructionism purport that the purpose of literary criticism is to deconstruct the meaning in art and the conventional understanding of said art. The seeming motivation underlying deconstructionism is the notion that most (perhaps all) art to date is somehow corrupt. Deconstructionism and analytic philosophy ostensibly share the view that our understanding of reality (through art and otherwise) is contaminated by biases, many/all of which are nefarious. From the perspective of Hegelism, by deconstructing (destroying) the meaning in art practitioners of deconstructionism are actually preventing knowledge (of the Absolute)—even stigmatizing this knowledge.

As to the concern that deconstructionism is required to confront such evils as racism and sexism in art, the case of Nazi cinema indicates that racism and sexism cannot be viably conveyed through art (chapter 2). More specifically, so-called art that conveys racism, and sexism is viewed by all as patently propaganda.

Turning the discussion to analytic philosophy, art (specifically Star Trek) conveys insights that challenge key analytic philosophy assumptions about the world. Central existential, philosophical issues, such as the human mind, aging (death), and the unpredictability of humans are forever outside of science. (These are all part of the pre-theoretical.) The ultimate argument is that humans must ponder and speculate about the Absolute (i.e., look beyond materialism) to gain an understanding (make sense) of the pre-theoretical (chapter 3).

Perhaps the key divide between continental and analytic philosophy is the issue of metaphysics (i.e., the nature of reality). Analytic philosophers hold that there is nothing outside of material reality. This turns us back to the question of the human mind and even life itself. Relying on later Star Trek, we can comprehend reality as an ontological process whereby the sum of objects make up more than their parts. The character of Lt. Cmdr. Data (*Next Generation*) explicitly embraces the idea that objects do represent more than their parts. The creation of Data (a life-form made entirely of inanimate materials) mirrors the creation of life from organic material (chapter 4).

Chapter 5 takes up the question of love. Hegel and Star Trek suggest that love of knowledge is superior to romantic love. This is in part because romantic love is about satisfying personal needs and desires—hence, it is on some basic level selfish. Love of knowledge is seemingly the highest form of love, because, ideally, it leads to a greater understanding of the Absolute. The creators of Star Trek take the critique of love further by holding that instrumental reason, like romantic love, is motivated by self-centered and ultimately dangerous impulses.

From popular culture we can observe that (criminal) justice is a dialectical process—with ideally the forces for vengeance and deterrence countervailed by the forces for the fair and judicious treatment of criminal suspects (chapter 6). The television series *The Man in the High Castle* and *Star Trek: Enterprise* indicate that the sacrifices the United States made in fighting World War II as well as the Cold War were for naught (as torture and authoritarianism are ostensibly ascending) (chapter 7). This is consonant with chapter 8, in which I demonstrate that shows like *Veep*, *House of Cards*, and *Game of Thrones* suggest that American democracy is in deep crisis—with politics dominated by personalities (not policy programs or the like); the public is seemingly disaffected from the democratic process; and the U.S. Congress is viewed as useless in dealing with pressing problems.

I'll conclude by invoking the installation of Donald J. Trump as U.S. president. The pessimism and demoralization I have highlighted in American popular culture leading up to 2016 can account for the political rise of Trump—someone who publicly and officially embraces racism, xenophobia, and even white supremacy.[1] Trump can be viewed as reflecting the political disaffection the public feels toward official politics—as reflected in such shows as *Veep*, etc.

NOTE

1. Alexander Burns, "Pushing Someone Rich, Trump Offers Himself," *New York Times*, June 17, 2015, A16; Sheryl Gay Stolberg and Brian M. Rosenthal, "White Nationalist Protest Leads to Deadly Violence," *New York Times*, August 13, 2017, A1; Michael D. Shear and Maggie Haberman, "Trump Again Says Two Sides at Fault in Rally Violence," *New York Times*, August 16, 2017, A1; Michael D. Shear, "Trump Imposes New Travel Ban on 7 Countries," *New York Times*, September 25, 2017, A1.

Bibliography

"About Those Black Sites," *New York Times*, Feb. 18, 2013, A16.

"After the Attacks: Bush's Remarks to Cabinet and Advisers," *New York Times*, September 13, 2001. Web.

Alderman, Liz. "Humans Wanted, but Robots Work," *New York Times*, April 17, 2018, B1.

Anderson, Terry H. *Bush's Wars* (New York: Oxford University Press, 2011).

Arbour, Brian. *Candidate-Centered Campaigns: Political Messages, Winning Personalities, and Personal Appeals* (New York: Palgrave Macmillan, 2014).

Bachrach, Susan, and Steven Luckert. *State of Deception: The Power of Nazi Propaganda* (Washington, DC: U.S. Holocaust Memorial Museum, 2009).

Bacon, Michael. *Richard Rorty: Pragmatism and Political Liberalism* (Lanham: Lexington Books, 2007).

Barilleaux, Ryan J., and Christopher S. Kelley, eds. *The Unitary Executive and the Modern Presidency* (College Station: Texas A&M University Press, 2010).

Bates, Jennifer Ann. *Hegel's Theory of Imagination* (Albany: State University of New York Press, 2004).

Bendersky, Joseph W. *Carl Schmitt: Theorist for the Reich* (Princeton: Princeton University Press, 1983).

Bernardi, Daniel. *Star Trek and History: Race-ing Toward a White Future* (Newark: Rutgers University Press, 1998).

Blackburn, Robin, ed. *An Unfinished Revolution: Karl Marx and Abraham Lincoln* (New York: Verso, 2011).

Bowman, Brady. *Hegel and the Metaphysics of Absolute Negativity* (Cambridge: Cambridge University Press, 2015).

Bronner, Stephen Eric. *Rosa Luxemburg: A Revolutionary for Our Times* (University Park: Pennsylvania State University Press, 1993).

Brownell, Kathryn Cramer. *Showbiz Politics: Hollywood in American Political Life* (Chapel Hill: University of North Carolina Press, 2014).

Burns, Alexander. "Pushing Someone Rich, Trump Offers Himself," *New York Times*, June 17, 2015, A16.

Burns, John F. "U.N. Panel To Assess Drone Use," *New York Times*, Jan. 25, 2013, A4.

Bytwerk, Randall L. *Bending Spines: The Propagandas of Nazi Germany and the German Democratic Republic* (Lansing: Michigan State University Press, 2004).

Cannon, James P. *The History of American Trotskyism: Report of a Participant* (New York: Pioneer Publishers, 1944).

Capaldi, Nicholas. *The Enlightenment Project in the Analytic Conversation* (Boston: Kluwer Academic Publishers, 1998).

Caplan, Jane. *Nazi Germany* (New York: Oxford University Press, 2008).

Carlson, Darren K. "Public Support for Military Draft Low," Gallup, Nov. 18, 2003. Web.

Carwardine, Richard, and Jay Sexton, eds. *The Global Lincoln* (New York: Oxford University Press, 2011).

Chatterjee, Pratap. "Our Drone War Burnout," *New York Times*, July 14, 2015, A21.

Chokshi, Niraj. "Robot Cures Human Headache: Putting Together Ikea Furniture," *New York Times*, April 19, 2018, B8.

Chomsky, Noam. *Language and Mind*, 3rd ed. (New York: Cambridge University Press, 2006).

Colaresi, Michael P. *Democracy Declassified: The Secrecy Dilemma in National Security* (New York: Oxford University Press, 2014).

Cortright, David, Rachel Fairhurst, and Kristen Wall, eds. *Drones and the Future of Armed Conflict: Ethical, Legal, and Strategic Implications* (Chicago: University of Chicago Press, 2015).

Critchley, Simon. *Continental Philosophy: A Very Short Introduction* (New York: Oxford University Press, 2001).

Critchley, Simon. *The Ethics of Deconstruction: Derrida and Levinas*, 3rd ed. (Edinburgh: Edinburgh University Press, 2014).

Dallek, Robert. *Lyndon B. Johnson: Portrait of a President* (New York: Oxford University Press, 2005).

"Dark Again After the Torture Report," *New York Times*, Dec. 12, 2014, A34.

Davey, Monica. "A Picture of Detroit Ruin, Street by Forlorn Street," *New York Times*, Feb. 18, 2014, A1.

Davis, Julie Hirschfeld. "'Deep State'? Until Now, It Was a Foreign Concept," *New York Times*, March 7, 2017, A19.

Desmond, William. *Art and the Absolute: A Study of Hegel's Aesthetics* (Albany: State University of New York Press, 1986).

Drape, Joe. "Bankruptcy for Ailing Detroit, but Prosperity for Its Teams," *New York Times*, Oct. 14, 2013, A1.

Drew, Christopher, and Dave Philipps. "Burnout Forces U.S. to Curtail Drone Flights," *New York Times*, June 17, 2015, A1.

Drolet, Jean-François. *American Neoconservatism: The Politics and Culture of a Reactionary Idealism* (New York: Columbia University Press, 2011).

Drury, Shadia B. *Leo Strauss and the American Right* (New York: St. Martin's Press, 1997).

Dudley, Will, ed. *Hegel and History* (Albany: State University of New York Press, 2009).

Duménil, Gérard, and Dominique Lévy. *Capital Resurgent: Roots of the Neoliberal Revolution*, trans. Derek Jeffers (Cambridge, MA: Harvard University Press, 2004).

Dyson, Stephen Benedict. *Otherworldly Politics: The International Relations of* Star Trek, *Game of Thrones, and* Battlestar Galactica (Baltimore: Johns Hopkins University Press, 2015).

"Effort to Prohibit Waterboarding Fails in House," Associated Press. March 12, 2008. Web.

Eldridge, Richard. *Beyond Representation: Philosophy and Poetic Imagination* (New York: Cambridge University Press, 2011).

Ellis, John Martin. *Against Deconstruction* (Princeton: Princeton University Press, 1989).

Fandos, Nicholas, and Sharon LaFraniere. "Two Reports on Meddling: Choose Your Own Verdict," *New York Times*, April 28, 2018, A14.

Feenberg, Andrew. *Technosystem: The Social Life of Reason* (Cambridge, MA: Harvard University Press, 2017).

Felski, Rita. *The Limits of Critique* (Chicago: The University of Chicago Press, 2015).

Ferrone, Vincenzo. *The Enlightenment: History of an Idea* (Princeton: Princeton University Press, 2015).

Fields, A. Belden. *Trotskyism and Maoism: Theory and Practice in France and the United States* (New York: Praeger, 1988).

Flegenheimer, Matt, and Scott Shane. "Bipartisan Voices Back U.S. Agencies on Russia Hacking," *New York Times*, Jan. 6, 2017, A1.

Frankfurt, Harry G. *The Reasons of Love* (Princeton: Princeton University Press, 2006).

Fukuyama, Francis. "After Neoconservatism," *New York Times Magazine*, February 19, 2006, 62.

Gallagher, Kelly Sims. *China Shifts Gears: Automakers, Oil, Pollution, and Development* (Cambridge, MA: MIT Press, 2006).

Gallagher, Mary Elizabeth. *Contagious Capitalism: Globalization and the Politics of Labor in China* (Princeton: Princeton University Press, 2005).

Garden, Ian. *The Third Reich's Celluloid War: Propaganda in Nazi Feature Films, Documentaries and Television* (Gloucestershire, UK: History Press, 2015).

Gardner, Lloyd C. *Killing Machine: The American Presidency in the Age of Drone Warfare* (New York: New Press, 2013).

George, Roger Z., and Harvey Rishikoff. *The National Security Enterprise: Navigating the Labyrinth* (Washington D.C.: Georgetown University Press, 2011).

Giglio, James N. *The Presidency of John F. Kennedy* (Lawrence: University of Kansas Press, 2006).

Glock, Hans-Johann. *What is Analytic Philosophy?* (New York: Cambridge University Press, 2008).

Goldberg, Michelle. "Trump Shows the World He's Putin's Lackey," *New York Times*, July 17, 2018, A21.

Gonzalez, George A. *The Politics of Star Trek: Justice, War, and the Future* (New York: Palgrave Macmillan, 2015).

Gonzalez, George A. *Energy and the Politics of the North Atlantic* (Albany: State University Press of New York, 2013).

Gonzalez, George A. *The Absolute and Star Trek* (New York: Palgrave Macmillan, 2017).

Gonzalez, George A. *Star Trek and the Politics of Globalism* (New York: Palgrave Macmillan, 2018).

Goodman, Peter S. "U.S. and Global Economies Slipping in Unison," *New York Times*, August 24, 2008, A1.

Goodman, Peter S. "Sweden Adds Human Touch to a Robotic Future," *New York Times*, December 28, 2017, A1.

Greven, David. *Gender and Sexuality in Star Trek: Allegories of Desire in the Television Series and Films* (Jefferson, NC: McFarland, 2009).

Gross, Neil. *Richard Rorty: The Making of an American Philosopher* (Chicago: University of Chicago Press, 2008).

Hafetz, Jonathan. "Don't Execute Those We Tortured," *New York Times*, Sept. 25, 2014, A31.

Halper, Stefan, and Jonathan Clarke. *America Alone: The Neo-Conservatives and the Global Order* (Cambridge: Cambridge University Press, 2004).

Hanley, Richard. *The Metaphysics of Star Trek* (New York: Basic, 1997).

Harootunian, Harry. *Marx After Marx: History and Time in the Expansion of Capitalism* (New York: Columbia University Press, 2015).

Harvey, David. *Seventeen Contradictions and the End of Capitalism* (New York: Oxford University Press, 2014).

Haverty-Stacke, Donna T. *Trotskyists on Trial: Free Speech and Political Persecution Since the Age of FDR* (New York: New York University Press, 2016).

Hegel, Georg Wilhelm Friedr. *Introductory Lectures on Aesthetics*, trans. Bernard Bosanquet (New York: Penguin, 1994).

Hegel, G. W. F. *Hegel's Aesthetics: Lectures on Fine Art*, vol. I, trans. T. M. Knox (New York: Oxford University Press, 1998).

Herf, Jeffrey. *The Jewish Enemy: Nazi Propaganda during World War II and the Holocaust* (Cambridge, MA: Belknap, 2008).

Hodgson, Godfrey. *JFK and LBJ: The Last Two Great Presidents* (New Haven: Yale University Press, 2015).

Hook, Sidney. *Towards the Understanding of Karl Marx* (New York: John Day, 1933).

Horkheimer, Max. *Critique of Instrumental Reason*, trans. Matthew O'Connell (New York: Verso, 2013).

Houlgate, Stephen. *Hegel's 'Phenomenology of Spirit': A Reader's Guide* (New York: Bloomsbury Academic, 2013).

Hurdle, Jon. "Philadelphia Forges Plan to Rebuild from Decay," *New York Times*, Jan. 1, 2014, B1.

Irwin, Neil. "The New Jobs Numbers Are Weaker than They Look," *New York Times*, July 2, 2015. Web.

Jacoby, Henry. *Game of Thrones and Philosophy: Logic Cuts Deeper Than Swords* (New York: Wiley, 2012).

Jones, Benjamin F., and Benjamin A. Olken, "Do Assassins Really Change History?" *New York Times*, April 12, 2015, SR12.

Jones, Daniel Stedman. *Masters of the Universe: Hayek, Friedman, and the Birth of Neoliberal Politics* (Princeton: Princeton University Press, 2012).

Jones, Gareth Stedman. *Karl Marx: Greatness and Illusion* (Cambridge, MA: Harvard University Press, 2016).

Kallis, Aristotle A. *Nazi Propaganda and the Second World War* (New York: Palgrave Macmillan, 2008).

Kaminsky, Jack. *Hegel on Art: An Interpretation of Hegel's Aesthetics* (Albany: State University of New York Press, 1962).

Kant, Immanuel. *Critique of Pure Reason*, trans. Max Muller (New York: Penguin, 2008 [1781]).

Kateb, George. *Lincoln's Political Thought* (Cambridge, MA: Harvard University Press, 2015).

Koistinen, David. *Confronting Decline: The Political Economy of Deindustrialization in Twentieth-Century New England* (Gainesville: University Press of Florida, 2013).

Kracauer, Siegfriend. *From Caligari to Hitler: A Psychological History of the German Film* (Princeton: Princeton University Press, 2004 [1947]).

Kreines, James. *Reason in the World: Hegel's Metaphysics and Its Philosophical Appeal* (New York: Oxford University Press, 2015).

Krugman, Paul. "Nonsense And Sensibility," *New York Times*, August 11, 2006, A15.

Krugman, Paul. "Robots and Robber Barons," *New York Times*, Dec. 10, 2012, A27.

Leonhardt, David. "We're Measuring the Economy All Wrong," *New York Times*, September 14, 2018. Web.

Lichtblau, Eric. "I.R.S. Expected to Stand Aside as Nonprofits Increase Role in 2016 Race," *New York Times*, July 6, 2015, A13.

Luke, Timothy W. *Shows of Force: Power, Politics, and Ideology in Art Exhibitions* (Durham: Duke University Press, 1992).

Machiavelli, Niccolo. *The Prince* (New York: Penguin, 2015 [1532]).

Mahler, Jonathan. "After the Imperial Presidency," *New York Times Magazine*, Nov. 9, 2008, MM42.

Maker, William, ed. *Hegel and Aesthetics* (Albany: State University of New York Press, 2000).

Malcolm, Noel, ed. *Thomas Hobbes: Leviathan* (New York: Oxford University Press, 2012 [1668]).

Manjoo, Farhad. "Uber's Business Model Could Change Your Work," *New York Times*, January 29, 2015, B1.

Marx, Karl. *On the Jewish Question*. 1844. Web.

Marx, Karl. *The Critique of the Gotha Programme* (London: Electric Book Co., 2001 [1875]). Web.

Marx, Karl. *Karl Marx on Colonialism and Modernization*, Shlomo Avineri, ed. (Garden City, NY: Doubleday, 1968).

Mazzetti, Mark. "'03 U.S. Memo Approved Harsh Interrogations," *New York Times*, April 2, 2008. Web.

Mazzetti, Mark. "Panel Faults C.I.A. Over Brutality Toward Terrorism Suspects," *New York Times*, Dec. 10, 2014, A1.

McGilvray, James. *Chomsky: Language, Mind, and Politics* (Cambridge: Polity, 1999).

McKee, Guin A. *The Problem of Jobs: Liberalism, Race, and Deindustrialization in Philadelphia* (Chicago: University of Chicago Press, 2009).

McPherson, James M. *Abraham Lincoln and the Second American Revolution* (New York: Oxford University Press, 1992).

Menand, Louis. *The Metaphysical Club* (New York: Farrar, Straus, and Giroux, 2001).

"Military Draft? Polls Finds Americans Opposed," Associated Press, June 24, 2005. Web.

Milkis, Sidney M. *Theodore Roosevelt, the Progressive Party, and the Transformation of American Democracy* (Lawrence: University of Kansas Press, 2009).

Miller, Carol Poh, and Robert Wheeler. *Cleveland: A Concise History* (Bloomington: Indiana University Press, 2009).

Miller, Claire Cain. "Smarter Robots Move Deeper into Workplace," *New York Times*, December 16, 2014, A1.

Miller, Claire Cain. "What's Really Killing Jobs? It's Automation, Not China," *New York Times*, December 22, 2016, A3.

"Mr. Trump and Mr. Putin, Best Frenemies," *New York Times*, June 29, 2018, A26.

Mumford, Stephen. *Metaphysics: A Very Short Introduction* (New York: Oxford University Press, 2012).

Myers, Constance Ashton. *The Prophet's Army: Trotskyists in America, 1928–1941* (Westport, CT: Greenwood Press, 1977).

Norton, Anne. *Leo Strauss and the Politics of American Empire* (New Haven: Yale University Press, 2004).

Norton, David L., and Mary F. Kille, eds. *Philosophies of Love* (Lanham, MD: Rowman & Littlefield, 1989).

Oakes, James. *Freedom National: The Destruction of Slavery in the United States* (New York: W.W. Norton & Company, 2012).

Olsen, Mary-Elizabeth. *Nazi Cinema as Entertainment: The Politics of Entertainment in the Third Reich* (Rochester, NY: Camden House, 2004).

Padgett, Deborah K., Benjamin F. Henwood, Sam J. Tsemberis. *Housing First: Ending Homelessness, Transforming Systems, and Changing Lives* (New York: Oxford University Press, 2015).

Palmer, Bryan D. *James P. Cannon and the Origins of the American Revolutionary Left, 1890–1928* (Urbana: University of Illinois Press, 2010).

Paolucci, Henry. "Introduction" in *Hegel: On the Arts*, Henry Paolucci, ed., 2nd ed. (Smyrna, DE: Griffon House, 2001).

Perkins, Robert L., ed., *History and System: Hegel's Philosophy of History* (Albany: State University of New York, 1984).

Pillow, Kirk. *Sublime Understanding: Aesthetic Reflection in Kant and Hegel* (Cambridge, MA: MIT Press, 2000).

Polk, Sam. "For the Love of Money," *New York Times*, Jan. 19, 2014, SR1.

Prados, John. *The Family Jewels: The CIA, Secrecy, and Presidential Power* (Austin: University of Texas Press, 2013).

Rancière, Jacques. *Aesthetics and Its Discontents*, trans. Steve Corcoran (Malden, MA: Polity, 2009).

Rappeport, Alan, and Thomas Kaplan, "A Battle to Protect Proposed Tax Breaks," *New York Times*, September 29, 2017, A16.

Redfield, Marc. *The Politics of Aesthetics: Nationalism, Gender, Romanticism* (Stanford: Stanford University Press, 2003).

Redfield, Marc. *Theory at Yale: The Strange Case of Deconstruction in America* (New York: Fordham University Press, 2016).

Rentschler, Eric. *The Ministry of Illusion: Nazi Cinema and Its Afterlife* (Cambridge, MA: Harvard University Press, 1996).

"Rewriting the Geneva Conventions," *New York Times*, August 14, 2006, A20.

Robbins, William G. *Colony and Empire: The Capitalist Transformation of the American West* (Lawrence: University Press of Kansas, 1994).

Robertson, John. *Enlightenment: A Very Short Introduction* (New York: Oxford University Press, 2015).

Rockmore, Tom. *Marx's Dream: From Capitalism to Communism* (Chicago: University of Chicago Press, 2018).

Rorty, Richard. *Philosophy and the Mirror of Nature* (Princeton: Princeton University Press, 1981).

Rutenberg, Jim, and Sheryl Gay Stolberg, "In Prime-Time Address, Bush Says Safety of U.S. Hinges on Iraq," *New York Times*, September 12, 2006. Web.

Rutter, Benjamin. *Hegel on the Modern Arts* (New York: Cambridge University Press, 2010).

Schecter, Darrow. *The Critique of Instrumental Reason from Weber to Habermas* (New York: Bloomsbury Academic, 2012).

Schmitt, Carl. *The Concept of the Political*, expanded ed. (Chicago: University of Chicago Press, 2007 [1929]).

Schulte-Sasse, Linda. *Entertaining the Third Reich: Illusions of Wholeness in Nazi Cinema* (Durham: Duke University Press, 1996).

Schwartz, Stephen P. *A Brief History of Analytic Philosophy: From Russell to Rawls* (West Sussex, UK: Wiley-Blackwell, 2012).

Seefedt Kristin S., and John D. Graham, *America's Poor and the Great Recession* (Bloomington: Indiana University Press, 2013).

Shane, Scott. "Waterboarding Used 266 Times on 2 Suspects," *New York Times*, April 20, 2009, A1.

Shane, Scott. "Portrayal of C.I.A. Torture in Bin Laden Film Reopens a Debate," *New York Times*, Dec. 13, 2012, A1.

Shane, Scott. "A Court to Vet Kill Lists," *New York Times*, Feb. 9, 2013, A1.

Shane, Scott. "U.S. Practiced Torture After 9/11, Nonpartisan Review Concludes," *New York Times*, April 16, 2013, A1.

Shanker, Thom. "Simple, Low-Cost Drones a Boost for U.S. Military," *New York Times*, Jan. 25, 2013, A12.

Shear, Michael D. "Trump Imposes New Travel Ban on 7 Countries," *New York Times*, September 25, 2017, A1.

Shear, Michael D., and Maggie Haberman. "Trump Again Says Two Sides at Fault in Rally Violence," *New York Times*, August 16, 2017, A1.

Singer, Irving. *Philosophy of Love: A Partial Summing-Up* (Cambridge, MA: MIT Press, 2011).

Singer, Peter. *Marx: A Very Short Introduction* (New York: Oxford University Press, 2001).

Slobodian, Quinn. *Globalists: The End of Empire and the Birth of Neoliberalism* (Cambridge, MA: Harvard University Press, 2018).

Smith, Steven B. "Leo Strauss: The Outlines of a Life," in *Cambridge Companion to Leo Strauss*, ed. Steven B. Smith (New York: Cambridge University Press, 2009).

Stevenson, Richard W. "White House says Prisoner Policy Set Humane Tone," *New York Times*, June 23, 2004, A1.

Stolberg, Sheryl Gay, and Brian M. Rosenthal. "White Nationalist Protest Leads to Deadly Violence," *New York Times*, August 13, 2017, A1.

Stolberg, Sheryl Gay, Nicholas Fandos, and Thomas Kaplan. "Measured Condemnation But No G.O.P. Plan to Act," *New York Times*, July 17, 2018, A1.

Strauss, Leo. "Notes on Carl Schmitt, *The Concept of the Political*," in *The Concept of the Political*, expanded ed., by Carl Schmitt (Chicago: University of Chicago Press, 2007 [1932]).

Street, Joe. *Dirty Harry's America: Clint Eastwood, Harry Callahan, and the Conservative Backlash* (Gainesville: University of Florida Press, 2016).

Sugrue, Thomas J. *The Origins of the Urban Crisis: Race and Inequality in Postwar Detroit* (Princeton, NJ: Princeton University Press, 2005).

Tanguay, Daniel. *Leo Strauss: An Intellectual Biography* (New Haven: Yale University Press, 2007).

Teachout, Zephyr. *Corruption in America: From Benjamin Franklin's Snuff Box to Citizens United* (Cambridge, MA: Harvard University Press, 2014).

"Ten States Still Have Fewer Jobs Since Recession," Reuters, March 25, 2016.

Tuck, Richard. *Hobbes: A Very Short Introduction* (New York: Oxford University Press, 2002).

Tufekci, Zeynep. "The Machines Are Coming," *New York Times*, April 19, 2015, SR4.

Uchitelle, Louis. "Goodbye, Production (and Maybe Innovation)." *New York Times*, Dec. 24, 2006, sec. 3 p. 4.

Unger, Craig. *The Fall of the House of Bush: The Untold Story of How a Band of True Believers Seized the Executive Branch, Started the Iraq War, and Still Imperils America's Future* (New York: Scribner, 2007).

Vaïsse, Justin. *Neoconservatism: The Biography of a Movement* (Cambridge, MA: Harvard University Press, 2010).

Van Natta, Jr., Don, Adam Liptak, and Clifford J. Levy. "The Miller Case: A Notebook, a Cause, a Jail Cell and a Deal," *New York Times*, Oct. 16, 2005, sec. 1, p. 1.

Vavreck, Lynn. "The Long Decline of Trust in Government, and Why That Can Be Patriotic," *New York Times*, July 3, 2015. Web.

Verene, Donald Phillip. *Hegel's Absolute: An Introduction to Reading the Phenomenology of Spirit* (Albany: State University New York Press, 2007).

Wachter, Susan M., and Kimberly A. Zeuli, eds. *Revitalizing American Cities* (Philadelphia: University of Pennsylvania Press, 2013).

Walsh, Declan, and Ihsanullan Tipu Mehsud. "Civilian Deaths in Drone Strikes Cited in Report," *New York Times*, Oct. 22, 2013, A1.

Wattenberg, Martin P. *The Rise of Candidate-Centered Politics: Presidential Elections of the 1980s* (Cambridge, MA: Harvard University Press, 1992).

Welch, David. *Propaganda and the German Cinema, 1933–1945* (New York: Oxford University Press, 2001).

Welch, David. *The Third Reich: Politics and Propaganda*, 2nd ed. (New York: Routledge, 2002).

Williams, Alex. "Robot-Proofing Your Child's Future," *New York Times*, December 14, 2017, D1.

Williams, Timothy. "For Shrinking Cities, Destruction Is a Path to Renewal," *New York Times*, Nov. 12, 2013, A15.

Willse, Craig. *The Value of Homelessness: Managing Surplus Life in the United States* (Minneapolis: University of Minnesota Press, 2015).

Wishon, Donovan, and Bernard Linsky, eds. *Acquaintance, Knowledge, and Logic: New Essays on Bertrand Russell's "The Problems of Philosophy"* (Sanford, CA: CSLI Publications, 2015).

Wolfers, Justin. "Congress and Us: A Hate-Love Relationship," *New York Times*, June 19, 2014. Web.

Wolraich, Michael. *Unreasonable Men: Theodore Roosevelt and the Republican Rebels Who Created Progressive Politics* (New York, St. Martin's Press, 2014).

Zee, A. *Einstein Gravity in a Nutshell* (Princeton: Princeton University Press, 2013).

Index

About the Author

George A. Gonzalez (Ph.D., University of Southern California, 1997) is Professor of Political Science at the University of Miami. He has been at the University of Miami since 1999. Prof. Gonzalez's area of research specialization is U.S. environmental politics and policy (e.g., energy, pollution, global warming). His books include: *Energy and Empire: The Politics of Nuclear and Solar Power in the United States* (2012, State University of New York Press); *Energy and the Politics of the North Atlantic* (2013, State University of New York Press); *American Empire and the Canadian Oil Sands* (2016, Palgrave Macmillan); as well as *Energy, the Modern State, and the American World System* (2018, State University of New York Press). Prof. Gonzalez has published research articles in *Polity* (the journal of the Northeastern Political Science Association). He has also published research articles in the journal of *Environmental Politics*, and in *Capitalism Nature Socialism*. In addition, Prof. Gonzalez has published original research in the journals *Studies in American Political Development* and *Public Integrity*.

Prof. Gonzalez also has a research agenda in the field of political theory and popular culture. In this area of study he has published articles in the journal *Foundation: The International Review of Science Fiction*, as well as the books *The Politics of Star Trek: Justice, War, and the Future* (2015, Palgrave Macmillan); *The Absolute and Star Trek* (2017, Palgrave Macmillan); *Star Trek and the Politics of Globalism* (2018, Palgrave Macmillan); and *Popular Culture and the Political Value of Neoliberalism* (2019, Lexington Books). Through the vehicle of the broadcast iterations of the Star Trek franchise, Prof. Gonzalez comments on metaphysics, international relations, justice, pragmatism, ethics, and the American left.

www.ingramcontent.com/pod-product-compliance
Lightning Source LLC
Chambersburg PA
CBHW022326280326
41932CB00010B/1244